What People Are Saying
No Limits, No B

Tiz Huch is a remarkable wife, mother, and copastor along with her husband Pastor Larry Huch. It's through her many life experiences and years of ministry that she reminds us of the timeless importance of prayer. Probably now more than ever, in a world full of chaos and pain, we must be reminded of the significance and power in praying God-anointed prayers. Tiz teaches us that prayer is not burdensome but freeing as she includes Scripture after Scripture of how to pray, when to pray, and what happens when we pray. It's time that we all include meaningful prayer in our lives daily as we commune with the One who created us and develop deeper relationships with our heavenly Father. After all, He is still a prayer-answering God!

—*Joni Lamb*
Cofounder, Vice President, and Executive Producer,
Daystar Television Network

No Limits, No Boundaries is a book written to help and instruct you to pray more effectively and to know that God does hear your prayers. He delights in answering the prayers of His children. It can be so easy to give up too soon in believing for our dreams to come true. But when we pray in faith and belief, God is always faithful. We can count on Him because we can know for a fact that Jesus hasn't changed, and He never will. I salute you, Tiz, and am so proud of you and Larry.

—*Dodie Osteen*
Cofounder, Lakewood Church, Houston, Texas

I am so excited about this book! Finally, a book that takes the religion out of prayer and makes it practical, purposeful, and powerful! If you've lost a sense of destiny, Tiz teaches you how prayer will help you find it again. I found freedom in the pages of *No Limits, No Boundaries*, and I know you will, too!

—*Martha Munizzi*
Award-winning singer/songwriter
International praise and worship leader

No Limits, No Boundaries by Pastor Tiz Huch is a brilliant outline straight from God's Word. What an incredible, truly enlightening revelation. I believe this book will impact the prayer lives of Christians from all walks of life. Through Pastor Tiz's precious hands, God has delivered a jewel to the world. Nothing is impossible with God!

—*Tommy Barnett*
Senior Pastor, Phoenix First Assembly of God, Phoenix, Arizona
Founder, The Dream Center, Los Angeles, California; Phoenix, Arizona; and New York, New York

What a powerful, insightful, and simple yet profound revelation. Pastor Tiz makes it plain and convincing that we can grab ahold of the promises of God through prayer. Her practical applications encourage the reader that this thing of promises and prayer is actually doable. This book is meaningful and yet an easy read for believers who are discouraged because of waiting for the promises of God. Take courage! This woman of God has a revelation that can make you a possessor.

—*Judy Jacobs*
Psalmist, author, teacher, and humanitarian

Pastor Tiz Huch is a breath of fresh air! I loved having her on my radio show—she brought such heartfelt joy and true wisdom for a hungry church. Her life is a powerful testimony of an intimate walk with the one true God.

—*Deborah Collins*
Host of *Celebrate Women Radio*

No Limits
No Boundaries

Praying dynamic change into your life, family, & finances

Tiz Huch

WHITAKER
HOUSE

No Limits, No Boundaries
Praying Dynamic Change into Your Life, Family, and Finances

Larry Huch Ministries
P.O. Box 610890
Dallas, TX 75261
www.newbeginnings.org

ISBN: 978-1-60374-119-4
Printed in the United States of America
© 2009 by Tiz Huch

Whitaker House
1030 Hunt Valley Circle
New Kensington, PA 15068
www.whitakerhouse.com

Library of Congress Cataloging-in-Publication Data

Huch, Tiz, 1956–
No limits, no boundaries / by Tiz Huch.
    p. cm.
    Summary: "Using the Lord's Prayer as a model, teaches readers the principles of powerful, effective prayer based on an intimate, trusting relationship with God"— Provided by publisher.
    ISBN 978-1-60374-119-4 (trade pbk. : alk. paper) 1. Prayer—Christianity. 2. Spiritual life—Christianity. 3. Lord's prayer—Criticism, interpretation, etc. I. Title.
BV210.3.H83 2009
242'.722—dc22

                        2009027539

2 3 4 5 6 7 8 9 10 11 12 🕮 17 16 15 14 13 12 11 10 09

DEDICATION

This book is dedicated, first of all, to my husband, Larry. You are my soul mate and my very best friend. For over thirty-three years, you have continued to astound me, inspire me, love me, encourage me, and spoil me! You are my greatest inspiration and my fearless leader!

Then, to my kids and their spouses, Anna and Brandin, Luke and Jen, and Katie. You have always shared in the dreams, passions, and journeys of our ministry. You have each grown and developed into an incredible adult with your own dreams and passions, both for our ministry and for your own life. You are the greatest treasures a mother could ever pray for, and the greatest family I could ever dream of. I'm so proud of you all!

Then, to my "Sugars" (my grandkids), Asher, Judah, and Aviva. You are the light and laughter of my life!

And then, to my parents, who have always been my greatest models of love, integrity, kindness, and perseverance. You will always be in my heart!

Also, to all of the "people for our life" who have been with us on this amazing journey. You make it possible for us to continue to achieve, enjoy, and keep reaching!

All of you are my gifts from God. Our best is yet to come!

FOREWORD

Tiz and I have been married for over three decades, and we have been in the ministry together for the entirety of our marriage. We have pioneered seven churches around the world, including two in Australia. We have done crusades and ministered in nearly every nation on earth. We have seen the Lord do incredible things over the span of our lives. Without a doubt, the Lord put our lives together. I never could have accomplished what I have in my own life without Tiz. Our marriage, our family, and our ministry are living testaments to the miraculous power of prayer!

Prayer has been the constant foundation of our lives, our family, our businesses, and our ministry. From the day that Tiz and I met as brand-new converts, we both have been people of prayer. We would spend hours on our knees in prayer, asking God to pour out His Spirit upon us and through us. In fact, seeing Tiz's passion for the Lord and her commitment to prayer was the second most important thing that drew me to her. I'll let you take a wild guess what the first thing was!

With a heart of passion and commitment, Tiz has stood by my side and prayed with me through our journeys and challenges over the past three decades. One of the greatest comforts in my life is the rock-solid foundation of prayer that Tiz and I stand upon. We know for a fact that we would not be where we are today without the miraculous power of prayer.

There are various keys to achieving success in our families, our ministries, our businesses, and our futures. But the most important keys to success are praying with power, hearing the voice of God, and then obeying and follow His leading. Prayer is the way we activate the promises of God, and it's a necessary key to success in every area of our lives.

One of Tiz's favorite sayings is, "A sermon is not just the message of an hour. It is the outflow of a life." This book is not only a book about prayer—it's a book about the outflow of our lives. Prayer isn't just something we do; it's who we are. To see the miracles and promises of God manifest as realities, you have to get them deep down in your heart. Through this book, Tiz will teach you how to possess the promises of God through prayer!

During a Sunday morning service several years ago, the Lord gave me several prophetic words for several members, and, for the first time, Tiz was among them! I'm always very cautious about giving words to my family or close friends, but this word was so strong that I called her out and prayed for her. The word from the Lord was that He was going to use her dynamically in the area of prayer. He was going to honor her for her heart and commitment to prayer for so many years. He was going to give her the gift of miracles and answered prayer. And He was also going to use her to teach about and release the anointing of prayer to others. God would honor her prayers at a new level and would take her into a new dimension of praying prayers anointed with the gift of miracles.

This word has come to pass in Tiz's life and ministry. She has always prayed intently for people and has seen supernatural breakthroughs, healings, and miracles. I've always said that she can pray and get people filled with the baptism of the Holy Spirit faster than anyone I know! Just as the Lord indicated to me, a new anointing for miracles has been released through her prayers. Let me put it this way: If I need a miracle, I want Tiz to pray for me!

In reading this book, not only will you discover teachings and stories from Tiz's heart, but you will also release God's anointing to pray with the same supernatural power as Tiz! If you want to learn how to pray with power and anointing, this is the book for you. If you're ready to see dynamic change come into your life, family, finances, and future, then this book is for you! If you're ready to live in the reality of all of God's promises, now is the time for your breakthrough! God bless you as you get ready for the journey of a lifetime!

—*Larry Huch*
Founder and Senior Pastor, DFW New Beginnings, Irving, Texas
Best-selling author, *Free at Last, 10 Curses That Block the Blessing*, and *The Torah Blessing*

Contents

INTRODUCTION

Architecture and interior design fascinate me, and I like to visit new home showcases, which are sometimes called Parade of Homes or Street of Dreams. These shows consist of streets lined with new homes constructed by prominent builders to exhibit their innovative designs and quality materials. I enjoy going to these shows to see the latest trends, be inspired, stretch my thinking, and enlarge my dreams.

Years ago, I was headed to one of these events with a few friends of mine. We were driving in a car, and as we came closer and closer to the area where the show was, we saw more and more signs and billboards that read, "Street of Dreams just ahead," or "You're almost there! Get ready for the Street of Dreams!" As we pulled in, I noticed a sign made of torn cardboard that was taped to a shabby-looking mailbox just across the street. On the sign was an arrow along with a handwritten note: "House of Reality...just down the back alley."

This image has since stuck with me as a vivid picture of the journey of life. We all have dreams about how we want our lives to be, but we're still living in a "real world" that is often quite different from those dreams. It is in the disillusionment of reality that we grow discouraged and get stuck.

Our frustration can often mount when we read the Bible and come across claims that seem contrary to the reality of life. We read about the life of our dreams—the abundant, fulfilling life God longs to give us (see, for example, John 10:10)—but we're living in the life of reality and disappointment. That's the reason I've written this book—to bridge the gap between our dreams, God's promises, and the realities of our present circumstances. Together, we are going to connect the dots of faith to see God's destiny established in every one of our lives!

WE ARE GOING TO ENTER INTO A NEW DIMENSION OF POSSESSING AND LIVING IN THE PROMISES OF GOD THROUGH PRAYER!

The primary purpose of this book is to open your eyes to a deeper understanding of how amazing and fabulous our God is! Then, my goal is to teach you how to access the wonderful promises that God has given to us, enabling us to tap into His endless supply of help, resources, favor, and grace. Through an intimate relationship with Him, and through an increasing knowledge of the promises He makes in His Word, we are going to enter into a new dimension of possessing and living in the promises of God through prayer!

Do you realize that God Himself wants to move through your prayers to change the circumstances of your life, your family, your finances, and the world around you? You're not the only one who wants your life and circumstances to change for the better. Your God wants them to change for the better, too! Even better news: He has mapped out simple and specific ways for you to accomplish this!

I know that the circumstances of life often make it seem as if the walls are closing in around us. We can feel overwhelmed by many responsibilities and pressures. Frequently, we feel like we're carrying the weight of the world all by ourselves, with no one to help us. I want to tell you right now that you are not alone. Not only that, but you have incredible amounts of help available to you, as well! No matter where you are in life, no matter how enormous your challenges are, and no matter how many times you think that you've messed up or failed, God is at this very moment thinking about you, planning out solutions for your life, and mapping out a fabulous, amazing future for you!

Jeremiah 29:11 says, *"For I know the thoughts that I think toward you,... thoughts of peace, and not of evil, to give you an expected end."* Think about that. God Himself has made plans for you—good plans, not evil plans! That's incredible, isn't it? We are on His mind right now! Psalm 115:12–13 says, *"The LORD hath been mindful of us: he will bless us...both small and great."* Without question, *God's desire for each of us is to bless us in every way and in every area of our lives!*

In the upcoming chapters, we will explore the nature of God and the assurance we have that He desires to bless and provide for us. One way that we will discover more about Him is by studying several of His names, which reveal His nature and characteristics—specific aspects of who He is and who He desires to be in our lives. Almighty God is a good, kind, loving, benevolent Father who watches over our lives with vigilance. As the psalmist wrote,

> *The LORD watches over you—the LORD is your shade at your right hand; the sun will not harm you by day, nor the moon by night. The LORD will keep you from all harm—he will watch over your life; the LORD will watch over your coming and going both now and forevermore.*　　　　　　　　　　　　　(Psalm 121:5–8 NIV)

This book is about praying without limits or boundaries. But even more, it is about the revelation of how amazing, awesome, and magnificent our God is, as well as how big He wants to be in us, for us, and through us! I want us all to come into a greater awareness of how good, loving, kind, and generous our Father really is. So, this book is not only about the act of prayer; it's also designed to reveal the true nature of the God to whom we pray. His names reveal His nature, which reveals His will and His desires for our lives.

You may be thinking, *If God is so good, then why am I facing so many struggles and obstacles in my life?* That's why the Lord has led you to this book! Before you or I even realize we are going to face a struggle, our Father has already mapped out a solution! Sometimes, the solution is just a prayer away. Sometimes, our answer is just a revelation away!

> SOMETIMES, THE SOLUTION IS JUST A PRAYER AWAY.

Often, when we're facing the enemy of our souls, we are totally unarmed and ill-equipped. This book will equip you with the necessary faith, knowledge, and understanding to seize the promises of God for the answers to your needs. Every step of the way, you will be transformed—from the inside out! As that transformation takes place, the miracles in your life will naturally begin to flow and multiply.

I'm going to show you Scripture after Scripture that establishes God's wonderful will and plans for your life. We will learn about and grasp the countless promises that God's Word contains for you, personally. Then, I will teach you how to live in that dimension of God's blessing—not just once in a while, but continually, until it becomes your lifestyle—through a dynamic prayer life modeled after the Lord's Prayer. I know for a fact that, as you read these chapters and take ownership of the promises of God, your mind, your heart, and your life will never be the same again!

THE LORD UNVEILS HIS WILL FOR YOUR LIFE THROUGH HIS WORD, WHICH IS YOUR GUIDE MAP.

As you absorb the Scriptures and discover God's desire and commitment to bless you, doubt and fear will no longer have a stronghold on your mind. The Lord unveils His will for your life through His Word, which is your guide map; when you follow it, you will launch forward into all of the incredible plans that God has designed for you! You will learn how to conquer every obstacle, cancel every plan of the enemy, and break every curse that has withheld blessings from you. Together, we are going to call in and release every single blessing that the enemy has ever stolen or held back, not only from your own life, but also from the lives of your family members for generations before you!

Together, we are going to grasp and hold on to every blessing that the Lord has promised to us! I'm going to teach you how to stop the enemy from sneaking back in, setting traps for you, and snatching away your blessings.

My deepest prayer is that all of your prayers will become realities. My dream is that all of your God-given dreams will come true. Close your eyes for a minute and imagine what your world would look like if it was completely filled with peace, joy, abundance, and health. Your "life of dreams" is about to become your "life of reality"! Come with me on the greatest adventure of your life—the adventure of praying with power and experiencing miracles!

TALKING WITH GOD

Chapter One

LIFE IS FRAGILE.
HANDLE WITH PRAYER.

Life is too fragile to simply leave in the hands of fate. I once saw a bumper sticker with the clever saying, "Life is fragile. Handle with prayer." What good advice! Through the course of this book, your thoughts, your words, and your lifestyle are going to move to a higher level. You and I are going to take a journey that will change our lives forever.

As I have said, the basis of seeing God's power moving in us, for us, and through us is knowing Him and His promises for us. When you know Him, are familiar with His nature, and understand what He desires for your life, it's easy to trust Him, because it's right here in the Book. When you read the promises of God, you see that God is a good, loving, generous, kind, big-hearted God. He's not a hard taskmaster. He's not a stingy God. He is a good God—all the time!

As you begin to understand and internalize this, you start to see your future differently. You see your future through the eyes of God, who has destined you to be successful in the plans He has for you. He's not up there waiting for you to make a mistake and then kick you when you're down. He is a good and loving Father who is in your corner, cheering and rooting for you. And He has the means and resources to ensure your success!

Prayer Gives Us Access to God's Limitless Resources

When you know that God believes in you, it changes the way you feel about yourself and transforms the way you approach life. It turns

> BECAUSE THE
> SPIRIT OF TRUTH
> DWELLS WITHIN
> US, WE CAN LIVE
> BEYOND THE
> LIMITATIONS
> OF OUR NATURAL
> TALENTS,
> ABILITIES,
> AND IQS.

impossibility thinking into possibility thinking, because we know that *"with God all things are possible"* (Matthew 19:26; Mark 10:27). It also changes the way that you view your own potential. Rather than thinking, *Oh, I could never do that*, or *That's beyond my abilities*, you begin to realize that God Almighty lives within you. Because the Spirit of truth dwells within us, we can live beyond the limitations of our own natural talents, abilities, creativity levels, and IQs. We have the opportunity every day to draw from the well that is within us and tap directly into the heart and mind of God Himself! The very God who spoke and formed the world lives within you and me. The moment we asked Him into our hearts and were born again, His Spirit took up residence and started living within us!

One of my favorite Scriptures is Ephesians 3:16–20. Paul was talking about being strengthened with might by God's Spirit in our *"inner man,"* that we might know *"the breadth, and length, and depth, and height"* of our God, who *"is able to do exceedingly abundantly above all that we ask or think, according to the power that worketh in us"* (verses 16, 18, 20). So, we see here that God's power is already alive and working within us and through us!

Romans 8:11 says that *"the Spirit of him who raised Jesus from the dead is living in [us]"* and *"will also give life to [our] mortal bodies through his Spirit, who lives in [us]"* (NIV). Do you grasp the significance of that? The same Spirit who raised Jesus from the dead and brought Him back to life is living within us. That same Spirit can raise us up in whatever way we need and enable us to do whatever He has put within our hearts to do!

That same resurrection power can break every chain, every bondage, every spirit of limitation or containment, every addiction, every emotional problem, every sickness, every disease, and every form of oppression or attack that tries to hold you captive.

We read in Daniel 11:32, *"The people that do know their God shall be strong, and do exploits."* *"The people that do know their God"*—that's you and I. Those of us who know our God will be strong and do world-shaking exploits! It's time that God's people live in the full and complete power of the resurrection!

Pull up the bucket from the well. That's where God is living. He's not way out there in la-la land or some distant universe; He is living inside of you. You have the ability to call upon His help, His strength, His wisdom, His riches, His creativity, His intelligence, His passion, His anointing—whatever you need, it's right there within you! Isn't that exciting? The fact that God Almighty lives and reigns within you and me is pretty amazing. What an incredible honor!

Prayer Activates the Promises of God

The blessings we're promised are not automatic, however. We have to ask for and activate God's promises through prayer. The Bible assures us over and over that the Lord sees and knows about all of our needs. Matthew 6:8, for example, says, *"Your Father knoweth what things ye have need of, before ye ask him."* But we still have to ask in faith to move His hand.

This process is similar to what happens when you receive a new credit card. You are given the card with full authorization and backing, but you still need to make a phone call in order to activate it before using it to make any purchases. In like fashion, God has sent His Word with full authorization and backing, but we still have to make the call to activate it! We have to ask!

The gospel of John confirms this idea. In John 14:12–14, Jesus said,

Truly, truly, I say to you, he who believes in Me, the works that I do shall he do also; and greater works than these shall he do; because I go to the Father. And whatever you ask in My name, that will I do, that the Father may be glorified in the Son. If you ask Me anything in My name, I will do it. (NASB)

The Lord never intended for His children to live within the confines and limitations of this natural world. His plan has always been to empower and equip us with His supernatural blessings—to add His "super" to our "natural." When we do our best, He will do the rest. But we have to ask!

Jesus Is Passing By—Seize Your Opportunity!

The tenth chapter of Mark includes the story of Bartimaeus, a blind beggar from Jericho. He sat by the roadside, day after day, appealing to the sympathies of passersby.

One day was different, however—Jesus came to Jericho. As He and His disciples were leaving the city, they passed by blind Bartimaeus, who shouted out, *"Jesus, thou son of David, have mercy on me"* (Mark 10:47).

Other people around Bartimaeus urged him to be quiet, but he shouted even more loudly, *"Thou son of David, have mercy on me"* (verse 48).

Because of the beggar's persistence, Jesus called Bartimaeus to Him and inquired, "What do you want Me to do for you?" (See verse 51.)

Bartimaeus answered, *"Lord, that I might receive my sight"* (verse 51).

The Bible says that he immediately received his sight, and Jesus Himself explained why. He told Bartimaeus, *"Go thy way; thy **faith** hath made thee whole"* (verse 52, emphasis added).

Bartimaeus was healed because he seized his opportunity and cried out, "Jesus! Don't pass me by! This is my moment. Heal my blind eyes!" The Bible records that Jesus heard his cry, stopped, saw his faith, granted his request, and healed him. How many other blind men did *not* cry out to Jesus and grab ahold of His promises by faith—and therefore missed out on their healing?

This account is an excellent example of how the spiritual realm operates. God knows our needs and sees our issues, but He can respond only to our faith and prayers. Let's never be guilty of letting Jesus pass us by and thereby missing an opportunity for a miracle. Jesus is passing by—let's seize our opportunity!

Are you ready to do as blind Bartimaeus did and lay hold of the miracles that the Lord has for you? I know you are!

Let's Begin Proclaiming God's Promises

Let's get ready to make some declarations together. When we boldly declare God's promises out loud, three powerful things happen:

1) We let God hear and know that we absolutely believe His promises for our lives.

2) We let ourselves hear and know that we absolutely believe God's promises for our lives.

3) We let Satan hear and know that we absolutely believe God's promises for our lives.

By declaring God's promises, we are putting God in His rightful place, putting Satan in his rightful place, and putting ourselves in our rightful places.

Ready? Speak this prayer out loud with me:

Father, I come to You through the name and the blood of Jesus. I thank You that You have called me to be more than a conqueror in every area of my life. I thank You that the same Spirit who raised Jesus from the dead is alive and working within me, and, therefore, that I can do all things through Christ Jesus who strengthens me. With You, Lord, nothing is impossible.

I declare that every spirit of darkness is broken off of my life and my family. Every generational curse is broken and reversed. Every bondage, chain, sickness, disease, or addiction is severed forevermore. The curse of poverty, insufficiency, and lack is bound from my finances from this moment on. Every spirit of limitation or containment is broken from my life and my future.

Now, Father, I release liberty, wholeness, happiness, and joy. I claim divine health over myself and my family. Thank You that the spirit of prosperity, increase, and abundance is being released into every area of my finances from this moment on. As for me and my house, there will be no limits and no boundaries! Thank You,

Lord, for complete and total victory in my mind, my spirit, my body, my life, and my future, and that Your plans and purposes are being released within me, for me, and through me, in Jesus' mighty name!

Now, give Him a big shout of praise and seal that prayer forevermore!

PRAYER AND PROMISE PRINCIPLES

- Knowing God and His promises for us is the basis of seeing His power move in us, for us, and through us.

- The Spirit of truth dwells within us, empowering us to live above the levels of our own abilities, talents, and IQs.

- Prayer gives us access to the limitless help, strength, and resources of our God.

- Prayer turns impossibilities into possibilities. (See Matthew 19:26.)

- God has destined you to be successful in every area of your life. He has the means and resources to ensure your success, and He has enabled you to access them through prayer.

- Our heavenly Father knows what we need before we ask.

- Boldly declaring the promises of God releases them into the realities of our lives.

Chapter Two

Prayer Puts Us on the Path to Blessing

From the beginning of time, God designed the world to be a wonderful, fulfilling, prosperous place where His children would live, enjoy the benefits of a covenant with Him, and accomplish His will for their lives. From the very beginning, God set up a covenant with His people—a covenant of blessing. Too often, people think of the old covenant—the law—as merely rules and regulations and legalism. The truth is that God's law is meant to be the path to all goodness and blessing! The enemy of our souls, the devil, works cunningly to paint an inaccurate picture of our God as a heartless taker and a hard taskmaster. But the truth is that our God is not a taker—He is a Giver! He is a good God!

We are the apple of God's eye. Our heavenly Father loves us with a deep, everlasting love, and He desires only the absolute best for His children! His love for us is so great that He sent Jesus, His only begotten Son, to die for our sins, thereby enabling us to have abundant life on this earth and eternal life in heaven. Understanding how much God loves us, cares for us, and desires to help us is vitally important because it is the foundation of all of our faith!

Jesus Himself gave us this promise in Luke 11:9–10:

Ask, and it shall be given you; seek, and ye shall find; knock, and it shall be opened unto you. For every one that asketh receiveth; and he that seeketh findeth; and to him that knocketh it shall be opened. (Luke 11:9–10)

WHY DO WE OFTEN MAKE THE BIGGEST PRAYER OF EACH DAY, "LORD, BLESS OUR MEAL"?

Let me ask you a question that I not only have asked thousands of others but also ask myself continually. If it is true that God really does hear our every prayer, and if He really is ready, willing, and able to turn every situation around, then why do we often make the biggest prayer of each day, "Lord, bless our meal"?

James 5:16 tells us that *"the effectual fervent prayer of a righteous man* [or woman] *availeth much."* In other words, our prayers carry great power! My fervent prayer is that every one of us would become more passionate about knowing God, reading His Word, and praying His promises. My goal is to help us to close the gap between what God has promised us in His Word and what we're experiencing as reality in our lives. I am absolutely convinced that many of God's children are living far below the standards that He intended for their lives. I believe that at this very moment, there are multitudes of miracles with our names on them, just waiting to be prayed into our lives. Let's not delay their arrival any longer!

Taking the Limits off of God—and Ourselves

In Ephesians 3:17–21, the apostle Paul expressed his heart's desire…

…that [we], *being rooted and grounded in love, may be able to comprehend with all saints what is the breadth, and length, and depth, and height; and to know the love of Christ, which passeth knowledge, that* [we] *might be filled with all the fulness of God. Now unto him that is able to do exceeding abundantly above all that we ask or think, according to the power that worketh in us, unto him be glory in the church by Christ Jesus throughout the ages, world without end.*

I love that Scripture because it challenges us to first take the limits off our perceptions of how big our God is, then to take the limits off of ourselves! There are no limits and no boundaries on what we are able to do because the limitless power of God is working through you and me. That's why prayer is so exciting! It connects us to who God is and to all that He wants to do in us, for us, and through us. By connecting God's super to our natural, prayer causes the supernatural to manifest in our lives!

As with any relationship, one of the most exciting things about our relationships with God is that there are always new dimensions and deeper levels to explore! The Lord has given us each an opportunity and an open door to know Him with increasing intimacy, to experience His presence more powerfully, to attain higher levels of His wisdom and knowledge, to walk in ever-increasing dimensions of His authority and dominion, to explore the depths of His hidden mysteries, and to place bigger faith-demands on His promises. As I have said before and will say again and again, there are no limits and no boundaries on what God can do! But we must make the choice to wade in deeper waters.

The Divine Exchange of Prayer

The Lord Himself designed prayer to be a means of creating a *divine exchange* through which we trade our natural strengths, abilities, and effectiveness—all of which are human and limited—for God's limitless power, abundant equipping, and all-sufficient, supernatural help. In my opinion, we're getting a pretty great deal! As I mentioned before, prayer is the channel God designed to apply His super to our natural. We exchange our limited resources and finances for His unlimited resources and provision, and He turbocharges, streamlines, and multiplies all of our labors, efforts, and time.

Prayer Lets Us Live on a Level above Fear and Worry

I like to tell people, "Worry and fear come when we view our futures without God in the picture." I also like to say, "Faith is fear that said its prayers." We can't control everything that happens in our lives, but we can control the way that it affects us.

> WE CAN'T CONTROL EVERYTHING THAT HAPPENS IN OUR LIVES, BUT WE CAN CONTROL THE WAY THAT IT AFFECTS US.

In each of our lives, there are many opportunities to become worried and fearful. Prayer is our way out of these negative emotions and circumstances. You and I are not meant to live under the circumstances of the world. We are meant to live by the promises in the Word. There is nothing as calming and empowering as speaking the promises of God over our minds, our lives, and our families. Hebrews 4:12 assures us that the Word of God is *"living and active"* (NIV). Yes, my friends, prayer changes things!

Changing the World through Prayer

In 2 Chronicles 7:14, the Lord opens a door of blessing to all of us, proclaiming, *"If my people, which are called by my name, shall humble themselves, and pray, and seek my face, and turn from their wicked ways; then will I hear from heaven, and will forgive their sin, and will heal their land."* Keep in mind that the word *"land"* is not just a term specific to the Israelites' property. Rather, it reaches to the farthest corners of the world, right down to the smallest details of our own lives! God has called you and me to stand in the gap between heaven and earth as people of prayer who connect the dots of faith between the Lord's promises and the realities of the world we live in.

What an incredibly powerful gift He has entrusted us with! Through prayer, you and I have the power to literally change the course of history, to drive back the forces of darkness, and to release the dominion and power of God into the entire world! That world includes nations and countries, states and cities, neighborhoods and schools, and, of course, our precious friends and families.

Not a Burden but a Burden Lifted

The realization that we are entrusted with the privilege and responsibility of praying for the world and bringing change through our prayers to the Lord can feel a little overwhelming, at times. Where are we supposed to start, and where are we supposed to end? Many people have the impression that prayer has to be burdensome, time-consuming, or heavy. The idea of prayer is often associated with deep, heavy soul-searching and repentance. These concepts can easily lead us to have an overall feeling of self-condemnation or cause us to experience clouds of heaviness and negative feelings that cast shadows on our lives. Deep, somber teachings on prayer often push people away from the regular practice of this all-important communion with God. You may have attended or heard about prayer meetings or similar events that were consumed with "travailing, weeping, and wailing." I know that such meetings occur, because I've been very involved with prayer ministry for more than thirty years, and I have heard many teachings on prayer and have participated in many types of prayers. I have had more than enough personal experiences with prayer intercessors at prayer meetings who have gotten a little off track—people who have become "so heavenly minded that they are no earthly good," to quote Oliver Wendell Holmes.

Don't get me wrong; I greatly value and appreciate anyone who has the desire, the heart, and the commitment to pray for extended periods of time as an intercessor. However, many times during our thirty-plus years in ministry, my husband, Larry, and I have had to "rein in" or realign good-hearted, well-meaning intercessors. As we ground them and guide them, their prayers become more focused and, therefore, increasingly powerful. In our dealings with people in these settings, they are usually relieved to find out that they can pray and see miraculous results without having to get "carried away," so to speak.

I want to disassociate prayer from feelings of being oppressed, overburdened, and weighed down. We will discuss repentance, soul-searching, and intercession in later chapters, but we don't want to get "stuck" there! Too much emphasis on these areas can create negative connotations and unproductive prayers, and can set us up to be robbed of so many blessings that the Lord wants to bring into our lives!

The Lord does not want to bring heavy burdens into our lives. He desires prayer to *remove* burdens, destroy yokes, and lift loads off our shoulders. Prayer is an incredible opportunity designed to be empowering, enlightening, illuminating, and exciting! It is an adventure into the limitless realms, levels, and depths of our amazing God. I want to teach you how to pray

> THE LORD DESIRES PRAYER TO REMOVE BURDENS, DESTROY YOKES, AND LIFT LOADS OFF OUR SHOULDERS.

in a way that will not leave you feeling sad and mournful but rather will invigorate, enliven, and empower you!

Again, we know that *"the effectual fervent prayer of a righteous man [or woman] availeth much"* (James 5:16). When we learn to pray with the power and anointing that God intends for us, we will see the miracles and breakthroughs that He has planned for us!

Achieving Results through Our Prayers

So, let's talk about how we can achieve powerful, life-altering results through our prayers. Let's shake off the heaviness that sometimes comes upon us at the mere mention of prayer and replace it with expectant anticipation, excitement, hope, and joy at the mere mention of prayer!

Get a Bigger Vision

I love to tell the story of the farmer who took his chickens out behind the barn, showed them a giant ostrich egg, and then told them, "Now, I don't want to put any pressure on you, but this is what others are doing!" That's what the Lord does with us. He takes us into the Word and shows us the giant "ostrich egg"—the tremendous promises that are available to us. Through these promises, He plants a bigger vision in our hearts and minds for us and for our futures. Along with a vision, He plants within us the hope and confidence that *"with God all things are possible"* (Matthew 19:26; Mark 10:27).

No matter where we are or what we find ourselves doing right now, God wants to outdo it! With God as our guide, life is a wonderful journey of outrageous adventures. And with His resources made completely available to us, there are no limits and no boundaries! Let's break away from the status quo—the chicken egg-sized reality—and grab ahold of an ostrich egg-sized vision for our lives! Our God is a big God with a big vision for each of our lives! Together, we are going to see every one of His plans accomplished in us, for us, and through us!

One of my favorite sayings is, "If we change our thinking, we will change our lives." The Word of God is supernatural. As you study it and pray it, allowing its truths to saturate your mind, heart, and spirit, it will take you on the journey of a lifetime—a journey of your dreams becoming your reality!

Don't Block the Blessings

Before we go any further, there is something else that's critical for you to grasp. The Bible tells us that there is one thing that can invalidate the Word of God and block the flow of His will and blessings in your life. According to Mark 7:13, man-made traditions that disregard the Word of God can prevent it from having any effect. In other words, our preconceived ideas, traditional thinking, or small-mindedness can cancel out the power of the Word to work in our lives. We don't want any old, unproductive, negative thinking to stand in the way of our blessings, do we? Of course not! So, let's open our hearts and minds to a fresh, new anointing from the Lord. Let's shake off that limited, traditional, skeptical thinking and let God stretch our minds and hearts. Let's break free from every small, puny, limited concept of our God and break into a new concept of how great, mighty, and powerful He really is!

> LET'S BREAK FREE FROM EVERY SMALL, PUNY, LIMITED CONCEPT OF OUR GOD AND BREAK INTO A NEW CONCEPT OF HOW GREAT, MIGHTY, AND POWERFUL HE REALLY IS!

Larry and I say this all the time: "The Bible does not say that the truth will set you free. It says that the truth you *know* will set you free!" I like to think of this principle in these terms: *The truth that you take ownership of will set you free!* The Word of God has been around a long time, and it will be around forever. However, it has the capacity to change our lives only if its truth and revelation penetrate deeply into our hearts and minds. We must take personal ownership of the Word and its promises. Then, we can begin to make demands, in faith, of the promises of God! When we do this, we will see the promises come out of the pages of the Bible and manifest as realities in our lives.

The Lord gives us the following promise in Isaiah 55:11: *"So shall my word be that goeth forth out of my mouth: it shall not return unto me void, but it shall accomplish that which I please, and it shall prosper in the thing whereto I sent it."* The Word of God states over and again that God is watching over His Word to perform it. So, we see that our God is ready, willing, and able to back up and bring to pass every promise that He has made to us in His Word! It's high time that we, as God's children, take Him at His word and begin learning how to activate His promises. Our God is ready, willing, and able, and I know that you are, too!

Prayer and Promise Principles

- God has a distinct, purposeful plan for your life.

- As you pursue your God-given purpose, you are never alone; God is always with you, giving you favor, grace, strength, and equipping.

- Take the limits off your perception of God, and take the limits off of yourself!

- There are multitudes of miracles with our names on them simply waiting for us to pray them into our lives.

- Prayer connects God's "super" to our "natural" so that the supernatural manifests in our lives.

- Through the divine exchange of prayer, we trade our own strengths, abilities, talents, skills, and resources for God's limitless power, abundant equipping, all-sufficient help, and divine wisdom.

- We have been entrusted with power to change the world through prayer, tearing down demonic strongholds on the earth and spreading God's dominion and authority all across the globe.

- Prayer is a privilege, not a burden, for it lifts troubles off our shoulders to be carried by God instead.

- Man-made traditions, doctrines, or skeptical thinking threaten to block the flow of God's blessings in our lives. Choose positive faith instead!

- God assures us that everything He has spoken in His Word will come to pass.

Chapter Three

A FOUNDATION OF INTIMACY

Knowing God, His nature, and His Word, which is His will, produces faith and boldness within us. Therefore, the bedrock foundation of powerful, confident, and effective prayers is having and developing an intimate, ongoing relationship with our heavenly Father. This type of relationship gives us the confidence to *"come boldly unto the throne of grace, that we may obtain mercy, and find grace to help in time of need,"* as we're exhorted to do in Hebrews 4:16. It is so important to realize that our God is inviting us to come into His throne room, where He will freely and willingly pour out His help, His mercy, and His grace. We often hear about God's throne of judgment, but we need to hear more about His throne of mercy, grace, favor, and unlimited help!

The key to answered prayer is knowing God and having an intimate relationship with Him that is built on the understanding that He is a good, kind, and loving Father who is always willing to hear us and help us. He created Adam and Eve for fellowship, and He wants the same kind of relationship with us: to walk with us and talk with us. He wants us to be constantly aware of His presence, to receive His love, and to express love back to Him.

In J. Oswald Sanders's book *Enjoying Intimacy with God*, he makes a statement that is both convicting and motivating. He says, "It is we, not God, who determine the degree of intimacy with Him that we enjoy. We are at this moment as close to God as we really choose to be."[1] Yes, I know that's a sobering thought—but let's not get stuck in self-condemnation! Instead, let's be encouraged and motivated to spend more time with the Lord! It's exciting to realize that, at any point in our lives, we can make a choice to draw closer to the Lord, who is waiting with open arms and listening ears. Let's be sure that we don't think of prayer as a duty for which we clock in and clock out, but rather as a privileged appointment with God Almighty.

> AT ANY POINT IN OUR LIVES, WE CAN MAKE A CHOICE TO DRAW CLOSER TO THE LORD, WHO IS WAITING WITH OPEN ARMS AND LISTENING EARS.

Getting to Know God

Let's look in the Psalms to discover more about the nature of our God and the type of relationship He desires to have with each of us. Psalm 37:4–5 says, *"Be delighted with the Lord. Then he will give you all your heart's desires. Commit everything you do to the Lord. Trust him to help you do it, and he will"* (TLB). Psalm 145:18–19 says, *"[God] is close to all who call on him sincerely. He fulfills the desires of those who reverence and trust him; he hears their cries for help and rescues them"* (TLB). What reassurance! As we purposely make the Lord out first priority, His throne room opens to us, and we come into a place of divine exchange.

Isaiah 40:31 tells us, *"They that wait upon the LORD shall renew their strength."* Another way of saying that is, "They that wait upon the Lord shall *exchange* their strength"—it's ours for His! You and I have the amazing privilege and opportunity of complete freedom of access to the King of Kings. We may freely enter into His presence and obtain help, strength, grace, and favor! The Lord Himself has offered us the opportunity to fellowship with Him and to have access to all of His eternal resources and abilities.

I think that if we really let that truth sink in, we would all spend a lot more time praying! I believe that we can accomplish more with twenty

---

[1] J. Oswald Sanders, *Enjoying Intimacy with God* (Grand Rapids, MI: Discovery House Publishers, 2000), 9.

minutes of prayer than with twenty hours of labor! If we really believe that God will answer our prayers, our biggest prayer of the day will not be, "Lord, please bless this meal." We will take seriously the opportunity and authority that He has imparted to us.

The second verse of the hymn "Come, My Soul, Thy Suit Prepare" by John Newton says,

> Thou art coming to a King;
> Large petitions with thee bring;
> For His grace and pow'r are such,
> None can ever ask too much.

He is a powerful, mighty God whose help is always available and whose resources are endless. What an amazing adventure we're on with Him! What an incredible privilege to be able to talk to Him, and then to have Him talk to us! As we pour our love into Him, He pours His love into us. Spending time in prayer and worship not only blesses the Lord, but it also blesses our own souls.

The Privilege of Sitting at the Feet of God

Over the years, I've had the honor of meeting many great people and world leaders involved in politics, business, or ministry. It has always fascinated me to watch and listen to people who have accomplished noteworthy things. I like to try absorbing some of their wisdom and knowledge as I listen to them speak. Just being in their presence is a great honor and a rare privilege that I never take for granted.

These special meetings are nothing, though, compared to the honor and privilege that you and I have every moment of every day to sit at the feet of God Almighty and talk to Him, listen to Him, and absorb the greatest wisdom and knowledge of all time! He is the ultimate Source of all wisdom, knowledge, strength, hope, creativity, understanding, and resources. And, He has allowed us complete access to all that He is and to all that He has! Wow! What an honor the Lord has given us! Doesn't that just lift you to a whole new level of excitement about your future? And then, on top of that, remember that it never ends! It's like climbing an endless ladder. Each new level leads to another new level, each one taking us closer and closer to our Maker and Redeemer. It is truly the never-ending story!

Our God Is a Good God!

Our God is a *good* God who loves us immeasurably. We need to saturate our thinking with the heart and mind of God, not the heart and mind of the enemy. I'm convinced that the enemy of our souls works to convince the world—and even God's people—that God is an angry, harsh, vengeful deity. Of course, we must not take God's judgment lightly, but His prevailing nature is not judgment; it's mercy and love for the people He created and redeemed! Let this truth sink into your heart: the Lord created Adam and Eve and then walked with them in the cool of the day. (See Genesis 3:8.) God Himself desired to fellowship with, have a relationship with, and hang out with His children! From the beginning of time, our God set up a covenant of blessing with His children that would flow out of an intimate relationship with Him. Of course, we know from John 3:16 that God loved us so much that He sent His own Son, Jesus, so that we, His children, could have life—and that more abundantly!

> AS THE SONS AND DAUGHTERS OF GOD, WE CAN HAVE COMPLETE, UNWAVERING TRUST IN OUR ABBA, WHICH GIVES US A PREVAILING SENSE OF PEACE AND ASSURANCE THAT HE HAS EVERYTHING UNDER CONTROL.

Cry Out, "Abba, Father!"

In the eighth chapter of Romans, Paul talked about what it means to be children of God. As God's children, we have received *"the Spirit of sonship. And by him we cry, 'Abba, Father'"* (Romans 8:15 NIV). The term *"Abba"* is an Aramaic word for "father," and it paints a picture of a young child trusting completely in his father to protect and take care of his every need. As the sons and daughters of God, we can have complete, unwavering trust in our *Abba*—our heavenly Father—which gives us a prevailing sense of peaceful assurance that He has everything under control.

When our children were young, Larry and I would buckle them in their car seats before we traveled anywhere. Today, we buckle in our children's children—our Grandsugars, as we call them. The children never asked, "Now, Dad, do we have enough gas in the tank? Have you checked the tire pressure? Did you adequately map out our route and calculate the approximate arrival time at our destination?" That would be unlikely coming from a young child! Little children just climb in their seats and enjoy the journey without worrying about the technical details of travel. They naturally trust that Mom and Dad have everything under control and are perfectly capable of getting them to the anticipated destination. This is the kind of trust that our heavenly Father wants us to put in Him! He is our loving, attentive, and fully capable Father who straps us in our car seats and drives safely with accurate directions. We can trust Him, relax, and enjoy the journey!

When Accepting God's Love Isn't Easy

Unfortunately, many people find it difficult to view God as a loving Father. Often, this difficulty stems from ugly, abusive experiences with their earthly fathers, which cause them to view all fathers, including our heavenly Father, as the opposite of kind and caring. This tainted impression of God can create major blocks to their trusting and receiving the blessings that the Lord wants to bring into their lives—and it can also perpetuate ugly, abusive behavior inflicted by the very people who suffered it as young children.

One Sunday morning, when Larry was preaching about the destructive force of anger, he was suddenly inspired to say, "I just feel like there are men here today who have never had a hug from their fathers and have never known what it is to feel a father's love. I know what that feels like." And then, he said, "I feel kind of corny saying this, but if you're a man who has never had a genuine hug from your father, I want you to come down here and let me give you a father's hug." The sea of men that flooded the altar was astounding! Nearly every man in the building came down to the front of the church. We were shocked to see hundreds of men of all ages and from every background and race weep as Larry hugged and prayed for them. As the men's tears flowed, the Lord healed many broken hearts and wounded spirits.

It is sad but true that many men and women around the world suffer the long-term effects of never having received genuine love from one or both of their parents. These individuals may appear at ease on the outside, but on the inside they have deep voids longing to be filled. The results of hurt and rejection can be far-reaching, and a crushed spirit can lead to many destructive behavior patterns. As we said before, emotional problems that aren't dealt with don't go away; they go underground, only to resurface months or years later. That is why it is crucial to deal with any emotional issues and to break the ties that they hold on us as early as possible.

Free at Last!

Larry's book *Free at Last* teaches truths from the Word that deal with generational curses, then reveals how to break these curses off of our lives and off of generations to come. This book was birthed out of our own personal experiences of generational curses and their effects, which nearly destroyed our marriage, our family, and our ministry. We know firsthand the strong power and destructive force of generational curses. More important, though, we know the incredible liberty, freedom, and blessings that come when we break those curses through the power of God! Once the curses have been broken and reversed, we release generational blessings, and everything the enemy had stolen from us is restored.

A parent's love and acceptance have a profound impact on the development and outcomes of a child's life. I grew up in a home where I knew that my parents loved me deeply. They expressed their love with words and actions alike, and I always knew that while my parents wanted me to succeed, they also accepted me for who I was, no matter what.

Our family wasn't perfect, but it was pretty close! When I became a Christian, I didn't have a problem believing that God loved me. I was able to accept and feel His love because of the love I had felt from my parents throughout my life.

Larry, on the other hand, had a more difficult time in the area of accepting love. He came from a rough, inner-city neighborhood full of violence. When he became a Christian, he was immediately set free and delivered from his addictions to alcohol, cigarettes, and drugs. His conversion was among the most dramatic and complete that I have ever seen. But a few problems lingered, including anger and violence, and this revealed to us the necessity of breaking the generational curses responsible for them. Larry tells people that his biggest obstacles were trusting God and accepting love from Him, as well as from other people. Because of his rough background, he struggled with feeling secure in God's love and faithfulness. When the Lord finally broke down those emotional walls and mental barriers, Larry's life was changed dramatically in every way. He was finally able to experience the peace, comfort, and rest that come from the love and acceptance of our heavenly Father. For more than thirty years now, we have experienced an increase of blessings in our marriage, in our family, in our ministry, and in every other area of our lives. When we free ourselves of the baggage of our pasts, God's love is able to flood our hearts and transform our lives.

> WHEN THE LORD FINALLY BROKE DOWN THOSE EMOTIONAL WALLS AND MENTAL BARRIERS, LARRY'S LIFE WAS CHANGED DRAMATICALLY IN EVERY WAY.

Larry's story is not unique; many other people in similar bondage have been set free from the generational curses that plague them and their families. The foundation of all that the Lord does for us, within us, and through us is built upon the rock of our loving relationship with God, our Father. What the Lord has done for us, we are committed to see Him do for others.

By the power of Jesus, Larry was delivered from the curse of his past. The following is an excerpt from his book *Free at Last* that I trust will help you better understand the concept of generational curses.

> Destructive personality traits and behavior patterns, addictions, suicidal tendencies, divorce, sickness, depression, anger, and dysfunction can usually be traced back through a person's family history. Statistics have shown, and it is now common knowledge, that a person who was physically or emotionally abused as a child has a

strong probability of becoming an abuser as an adult. Children of alcoholics who hated their parents' behavior often become alcoholics themselves, and the list of examples goes on.

A sad example of this is the child who has been physically or sexually abused. This child has gone through the turmoil, heartache, and pain of being abused by a parent or a relative. You would think that a person who has suffered the trauma of such abuse would be the last one to inflict that horror on someone else. However, that individual is very likely to become a child abuser or, if not an abuser, to become angry and self-destructive. Why? The spirit of iniquity—the thing that drives them to do what they know they're not supposed to do—is passed down from generation to generation.

Generational curses—curses that are handed down from family member to family member, generation after generation—have been around since Adam's disobedience. Who was the first sinner? Adam. Who was the first murderer in the Bible? Adam's son, Cain. Who was the second murderer? Cain's descendant, Lamech. Why? Because of the iniquity that passed down through the generations of Adam's offspring. (See Genesis 4:8, 23.)

Family curses, generational curses, the iniquity of parents passed down to the third and fourth generation....Sound depressing and hopeless? It's not. Every time the devil brings a problem, Jesus has already brought an answer!

We have an example of hope in Rahab the harlot. Rahab was a Canaanite woman whose house was on the wall of Jericho. Many of us have read Joshua 6 and know the wall of Jericho came tumbling down after the children of Israel marched around it seven times as God directed. As a result, the entire city of Jericho was destroyed except Rahab and her family. Because she had hidden the Hebrew men who came to spy out the land of Canaan before they entered the Promised Land, Rahab was spared along with her family and *"all that she had"* (Joshua 6:25). As a Canaanite, Rahab was under the curse of the Canaanites that began generations earlier when

Noah got drunk and his son Ham *"saw the nakedness of his father"* (Genesis 9:22). Whatever perverse act occurred while Noah was drunk, in the end Noah declared that Canaan, Ham's son, was cursed. (See Genesis 9:18–25.) Rahab broke the curse that was on her family through their ancestor Canaan by sparing the lives of the men of God. The cord of scarlet Rahab put in her window when Israel attacked was a symbol of the delivering power of the blood of Jesus. (See Joshua 2:14–21.)

Just like Rahab, you can break the curse on your family. You can bless your family. That curse started somewhere and it can end somewhere.[2]

When we have been abused emotionally or physically by people we love, it creates a wall of hurt and mistrust around our hearts. We have to allow the Holy Spirit to break down those walls to let the love of our Father flow in and heal our hearts. Only an encounter with Jesus Christ was able to give Larry the peace and freedom he had longed for. Only the power of the Holy Spirit could give him the deliverance he needed to live the life he had dreamed of. More than thirty years ago, Larry met the Son of God, and his life was drastically changed forevermore! For the decades since that day, he and I have been telling people around the world that what the Lord has done for us, He will also do for them. And He'll do it for you, too!

Peace Prevails in a Violent Life

Another example of a life freed from a generational curse is a friend of ours named Shelley. When we met Shelley, she told us that she had grown up in a very violent home. She said that her dad would hit her mom, who would then hit her children. Unfortunately, that's a pretty common scenario.

Shelley explained to me that her parents would tell her that she was loved, but that she was a terrible child who would never amount to anything. This type of environment caused her to grow up into an angry, bitter, and hateful person. She was resentful of her parents, her brothers and sisters, and basically anyone who crossed her path.

---

[2] Larry Huch, *Free at Last* (New Kensington, PA: Whitaker House, 2000, 2003, 2004), 31–34.

Shelley became involved with a man named Rod, and it isn't surprising that he was violent and abusive, just like her parents. Because she had never known life without abusive relationships, she went ahead and married him. Naturally, things went from bad to worse. Drugs became a daily part of life. Arguing and knock-down, drag-out fights became a common occurrence. When Shelley and Rod had children, the violence spilled into their lives, as well.

One day, someone invited Shelley and Rod to our church, New Beginnings. Not knowing what to expect but having nothing to lose, they came. The morning of their visit, after Shelley and Rod heard the life-changing message of the gospel for the first time ever, they ran to the altar and gave their lives to the Lord. Larry and I prayed for them and broke the curses over their lives.

From that moment on, they were both changed from the inside out! They became involved in our Overcomers Ministry and learned how to break free from the spiritual bondages that had long held them captive.

They also learned how to change negative behavior patterns and habits, and managed to create an entirely new outlook on life. Not only was their marriage healed, but their relationships with their children were healed, as well. For years now, they have been involved in the church, helping others to find the same freedom and joy that the Lord brought to them. Shelley told me that her biggest breakthrough was when she was able to accept and experience the love of her heavenly Father. As the love of God became real and tangible to her, all of the emotional baggage from her past began to subside, and the wall she had built around her heart began to crumble. She said that when she really understood that God loved her, she felt like the weight of the world had been lifted off of her. She knew she wasn't alone anymore.

Just as the Lord changed Shelley and transformed her life with His love, He can change you or someone you love. Our Father is a good, kind, compassionate, and powerful God whose love can truly change the world—including your own life.

PRAYER AND PROMISE PRINCIPLES

- Intimacy with our heavenly Father is the foundation of powerful, confident, and effective prayers.

- We have the incredible honor of being able to commune with God and absorb His wisdom and knowledge through spending time with Him, reading His Word, and praying to Him.

- Our Father has everything under control, and we can trust Him completely with our lives, our families, and our futures.

- It is difficult for those whose earthly fathers were abusive or unloving in the treatment of their children to view God as a loving Father.

- God's love and power can break generational curses, shatter demonic strongholds, and radically transform lives. By breaking generational curses or patterns in our lives, we can be free to give and receive love.

Chapter Four

COMMUNING WITH OUR FATHER

It can be difficult to fathom the fact that God takes pleasure in spending time with us. Seriously, why would He want to commune with us flawed and fallen human beings? There have probably been seasons in all of our lives when few people wanted to be around us. At one time or another, most of us have experienced feeling unwanted, unaccepted, or unloved. And, if we're truthful, sometimes we aren't exactly lovable, are we? If our friends and family members occasionally don't even want to be with us, why would God Almighty want to hang out with us? The Lord only knows—but He surely does. Even if nobody else in the entire world wants to have a thing to do with us, our Father wants everything to do with us!

God's Door Is Always Open

One day, I was in my office at the church preparing my notes for the service. I had my door shut so that I wouldn't be disturbed and could focus my thoughts. All of a sudden, I heard giggling and a *scratch, scratch* on the door. I looked up to see my four-year-old twin Grandsugars, Asher and Judah, peaking in through the door with great big smiles, impatient for me to see them! To everyone else, my door was shut, but to my Sugars, there's never a closed door! I dropped everything and ran to them for my hugs and my kisses. At that moment, nothing in the world was more important to me than loving and being loved by my Sugars!

> WE ARE THE
> LIGHTS OF GOD'S
> LIFE. HE'S JUST
> WAITING FOR US
> TO COME ON IN
> AND SPEND SOME
> TIME WITH HIM!

And it's the same way with God. His door is never shut to us, His "Sugars." He'll drop everything when you come and peek in His door! Just like those Sugars are the light of my life, we are the lights of God's life. He's just waiting for us to come on in and spend some time with Him! So, when you go before Him, express from your heart—and feel in return from His heart—joy, love, peace, pleasure, and acceptance. Just enjoy each other!

We Are Offered a Relationship of Intimacy with Our Creator

As we've already discussed, intimacy with the Lord, which comes from worshipping Him with our hearts, is the foundation of learning to pray with power. It's like the top button on a button-down shirt—if you don't get the top one buttoned right, none of the other buttons will line up. But when you match the top button to the correct buttonhole, everything else lines up perfectly and easily! We probably all know the Scripture I'm about to share, but let's take a fresh look at it and make it our own.

> *Blessed is the man that walketh not in the counsel of the ungodly, nor standeth in the way of sinners, nor sitteth in the seat of the scornful. But his delight is in the law of the LORD; and in his law doth he meditate day and night. And he shall be like a tree planted by the rivers of water, that bringeth forth his fruit in his season; his leaf also shall not wither; and whatsoever he doeth shall prosper.* (Psalm 1:1–3)

What a picture of continual blessing, joy, and abundance! When we simply make the Lord and His Word the top priority and the starting point—the top button—of our lives, whatever we do shall prosper! This begins with worship, which isn't restricted to the songs we sing in church on Sundays; no, worship is a lifestyle that involves continually acknowledging God's greatness and living to bring Him glory.

We Are Invited to Partner with God through Prayer

It truly amazes me that God Himself desires to move through our prayers to change the circumstances of our lives, our families, our finances, and our futures. So often, we have the misconception that prayer is just about pleading our cases before God or begging Him to meet our basic needs. But prayer was not established primarily as a means for desperate people to plead for God's help. When Jesus taught His disciples to pray, He gave them a model that involved, first and foremost, praise and adoration for the Lord (see, for example, Matthew 6:9), followed by a supplication for His will to be done (see, for example, Matthew 6:10).

FROM THE BEGINNING OF TIME, GOD HAS INTENDED FOR PRAYER TO BE HIS MEANS OF MOVING HIS PROMISES OUT OF THE PAGES OF THE BIBLE AND INTO THE REALITIES OF OUR LIVES!

The Lord has ordained for you and me to pray His will into this world, into our own lives, and into the lives of our family members. Prayer has always been the channel through which we come to know God by communicating with Him, as well as obtain His help in times of need, connect His super to our natural, and establish His dominion in our lives, our families, and in the world. From the beginning of time, God has intended for prayer to be His means of moving His promises out of the pages of the Bible and into the realities of our lives! Prayer is something God designed for us to use in order to possess His promises.

Many Are Called; Few Are Chosen

Have you ever wondered about the significance of the Scripture that says, *"Many are called, but few are chosen"* (Matthew 22:14)? At first glance, it almost sounds like it's talking about an exclusive club for a chosen few. Of course, there are many layers of significance to this Scripture, but I believe that one primary meaning is that God does not show partiality. (See Acts 10:34 NKJV, NASB.) I believe that the Lord extends a call to everyone to draw closer to Him, to proclaim more of His promises, and to walk through His open door to experience the fullness of all that He is and all that He wants to do in us, for us, and through us. *"Many are called"* through the open door to God's blessings.

However, not everyone responds to this call. The few who are chosen are the ones who answer the call and accept God's offer. God makes His move; then the ball is in our court! It's up to us to respond in faith by accepting Christ in our hearts and acting as His children. In doing this, we *become* the "chosen ones." With this freedom of choice, though, comes the option of ignoring God's invitation and thereby being excluded from the "chosen ones." I don't want this to sound ominous, but the truth is that our futures are determined by the choices that we make. Many people don't want to take responsibility for their futures. It's much easier just to hang out, hang on, and hope for the best.

> GOD HAS PUT YOU IN THE PLACE WHERE YOU ARE, AT THIS PARTICULAR TIME, FOR A SPECIFIC PURPOSE!

We need to realize that today's decisions determine tomorrow's destiny! To me, the fact that my choices have consequences does not fill me with dread. It's exciting and empowering to realize that I can play an active part in changing my future, that I don't have to be a victim of any negative circumstances of life, and that I can, by my choices, become a chosen one of God! Always keep in mind the fact that today's choices determine tomorrow's destiny, and allow this thought to be a source of excitement and motivation for you. God has put you in the place where you are, at this particular time, for a specific purpose! He has destined you to move into an entirely new dimension in your spiritual walk with Him and in your natural life on this earth. So, embrace the responsibility to make wise decisions, and begin with the decision to become a chosen one of God! John 1:12 says that *"to all who received [Jesus], to those who believed in his name, he gave the right to become children of God"* (NIV).

Let's discuss some of the exciting implications of being a child of God—one of His chosen few.

We Can Come Boldly to the Throne of Grace!

The Bible tells us to come boldly to the throne of grace to receive help in times of need. I like the *Amplified Bible* translation of Hebrews 4:16:

Let us then fearlessly and confidently and boldly draw near to the throne of grace (the throne of God's unmerited favor to us sinners), that we may receive mercy [for our failures] and find grace to help in good time for every need [appropriate help and well-timed help, coming just when we need it].

It's not a throne of judgment; it's a throne of grace! There, we find nothing but His love, acceptance, mercy, grace, and favor.

Let's return to the Scripture that tells us that *"many are called, but few are chosen"* (Matthew 22:14). We talked about how the Lord makes this elite status—the status of a chosen one—available to every person. Only those who respond to that call, however, go on to become the chosen ones. Always keep in mind that the Lord is ready, willing, and able to give us salvation, dwell within us, hear our prayers, and have a personal relationship with us. He has an open door to Himself that He's just waiting for us to walk through!

With God, there is no discrimination or favoritism. There are no security doors to keep us out of His offices or His throne room. There are no exclusive levels of faith that allow access only to a chosen few. Every one of us has equal access to the throne of God! Our Father has opened the door to each of us who desires to enter in. We are in His elite circle! What an incredible privilege!

We Are on His Mind Right Now!

Often, when we pray, we seem to position ourselves as beggars supplicating God to bless us, help us, or heal us. We feel that we have to plead our cases to get Him to move on our behalf. The truth of the matter, however, is that God *desires* to intervene and help us—we don't have to convince Him to do so! The Lord doesn't want us to come to Him with the mind-set of an unworthy beggar. He wants us to come fully persuaded of His goodness and willingness to help us, His children. He wants us to stand before Him in complete confidence and faith!

We're not to plead as beggars; we are simply to acknowledge who God is and what He has already done for us. God desires for us to succeed in every plan He has put into our lives. He has destined us to win, and He

> GOD DESIRES FOR US TO SUCCEED IN EVERY PLAN HE HAS PUT INTO OUR LIVES. HE HAS DESTINED US TO WIN, AND HE HAS DESIGNED A PLAN FOR EACH OF US TO ACCOMPLISH HIS PURPOSES FOR OUR LIVES.

has designed a plan for each of us to accomplish His purposes for our lives.

Psalm 115:12 assures us that *"the Lord hath been mindful of us: he will bless us."* In other words, we are on His mind; right this very minute, you are on His mind! He is mindful—or aware—of our situations and circumstances. He is tuned in and plugged in! Not only is He aware of our situations, but He has already worked out a plan to bless us beyond measure. Now that is worth shouting about!

God Is in Our Corner, Cheering Us On!

My hope is that every person knows how it feels to have someone cheering him on. Think of the surge of encouragement we experienced when, for example, a parent cheered for us from the sidelines of our childhood soccer games or tennis matches. The support of fans is important not only in sports, the performing arts, and other similar realms, but also in our day-to-day existence as we stride through or struggle through the obstacle course called life. Whether it's been a loving parent encouraging you to step out into new areas of experience, a teacher challenging you to rise to higher levels of scholarship, or a coach believing that you can set a record or make that game-saving goal, the presence of an individual who cheers you on adds exhilaration and energy to your pursuit, doesn't it? When you know that someone is in your corner, cheering you on and assisting you, it gives you the feeling that you can take on the world!

Whether or not you have experienced the empowerment of a cheering fan, you are about to feel it from the Lord! He is in your corner, cheering you on! He believes in you! And furthermore, He will equip and enable you to accomplish every God-given pursuit that you set your mind to! Remember, *"Delight yourself in the Lord and he will give you the desires of your heart"* (Psalm 37:4 NIV). If you allow Him to, He will lead you into a destiny beyond your wildest dreams!

A friend of mine who attends our church started a small company, a venture that, as you probably know, entails many challenges. One day, after she had broken through some of the barriers she had been facing, she said to me, "Thank you for seeing in me what I couldn't see in myself."

You see, when we're in the midst of fighting our battles, it's sometimes hard to see ourselves coming out on the winning side. All we can see are the barriers blocking the blessing and our own limitations or lack of abilities or resources. Down and discouraged, we long for someone to believe in us and encourage us. Thank God if we have someone in our lives who provides the encouragement we need—but that isn't true of everybody. Whether or not you have a friend or family member to be the "cheerleader" in your life, your heavenly Father believes in you, and He is cheering you on in all that you do! When God is on your side and in your corner, nothing is too hard or impossible! *"If God be for us, who can be against us?"* (Romans 8:31). I know that you believe in God—now, believe that He believes in you!

> WHETHER OR NOT YOU HAVE A FRIEND OR FAMILY MEMBER TO BE THE "CHEERLEADER" IN YOUR LIFE, YOUR HEAVENLY FATHER BELIEVES IN YOU, AND HE IS CHEERING YOU ON IN ALL THAT YOU DO!

Not only does God believe in you, but He is also proud of you. After all, you and I, *"we are God's workmanship, created in Christ Jesus to do good works, which God prepared in advance for us to do"* (Ephesians 2:10 NIV). Every time we seek to obey our heavenly Father and fulfill His purposes for our lives, we make Him extremely proud.

Other people may have given up on you, or maybe you've given up on yourself. But the Lord hasn't given up on you—nor will He ever! Even if you feel like the whole world is against you, your Father is pulling for you! No matter how many times we have messed up or failed, our God never counts us out! He gives us hope when nobody else will give us a prayer. He gives us

> GOD'S PLAN IS NOT TO CONDEMN US BUT RATHER TO SAVE US. IT WAS NO SMALL SACRIFICE HE MADE. GOD SENT HIS ONLY SON—HIS PERFECT, RIGHTEOUS SON—TO BEAR THE SHAME, PAY THE PRICE, AND ULTIMATELY DIE FOR OUR SINS.

a written plan when others have written us off. Today is a great day to shake off every burden or chain from your past and to start fresh with freedom in the Lord! This is your day to make a brand-new beginning!

God's Son Jesus Paid Our Debt

I know that it can be difficult to comprehend just how much God loves us, especially if we have had few past experiences of true human love and acceptance. It's critical that we let the fact of God's love settle deeply within our hearts and minds. John 3:16–17 says, *"For God so loved the world that he gave his one and only Son, that whoever believes in him shall not perish but have eternal life. For God did not send his Son into the world to condemn the world, but to save the world through him"* (NIV).

We see here that God's plan is not to condemn us but rather to save us. It was no small sacrifice He made. God sent His *only* Son—His perfect, righteous Son—to bear the shame, pay the price, and ultimately *die* for our sins. Do you realize how deeply He loves you and me? Ephesians 2:4–7 says this:

> But God, who is rich in mercy, because of His great love with which He loved us, even when we were dead in trespasses, made us alive together with Christ (by grace you have been saved), and raised us up together, and made us sit together in the heavenly places in Christ Jesus, that in the ages to come He might show the exceeding riches of His grace in His kindness toward us in Christ Jesus. (NKJV)

Our Father willingly sent His own Son to be whipped, beaten, scorned, bruised, nailed to a cross, and ultimately to die—a flawless sacrifice for us, fallen and flawed sinners—so that we could have eternal life in heaven and also abundant, blessed, and whole lives on earth. As a parent, I can't even imagine making that kind of sacrifice. What incomprehensible, amazing love our Father has for us! Nobody else has ever loved us like that, and nobody else *could* ever love us like that! Right now, take a minute to close your eyes and thank God for His love. Just allow His love to saturate your heart and your soul. That's a great feeling, isn't it?

PRAYER AND PROMISE PRINCIPLES

- As God's children, we each have equal access to His throne of grace.
- God's door is always open to us, and we can approach Him with confidence and present our requests boldly.
- Cultivating an intimate relationship with God causes everything else to line up according to His purposes.
- Worship is the foundation of an intimate relationship with God.
- God designed prayer to be a means by which we move His promises out from the pages of the Bible and into the realities of our lives in the world.
- God Himself desires to move through our prayers to change our lives, families, finances, and futures.
- We are on God's mind right now!
- Our heavenly Father is our biggest fan!
- God's love can be hard to fathom, but we can sense its amazing magnitude by thinking about His act of sending His Son as a sacrifice to die for us so that we may have life.
- If God is for us, who can be against us?

Chapter Five

Prayer Is a Two-Way Conversation

A good friend of ours from church, Gerald, is a successful business-man who was presented with the opportunity to take over an existing company. He later told us that while he felt that it could be an incredibly lucrative venture, he had no idea of how to make it happen. He didn't have the finances to pull it together. In his heart, though, he still felt that the Lord was leading him toward this opportunity. So, he prayed and asked Him to direct his thoughts and steps.

He explained to us how in church one Sunday morning, he was worshipping the Lord with his eyes closed, praising God for His love and goodness, when suddenly in his mind he saw the whole plan clearly laid out. He remembered several previous contacts who could assist him with financing, and he thought of certain professionals who would make compatible business partners. He visualized the timetable to make it happen, and he felt complete confidence that this was an opportunity from the Lord.

Over the next few weeks, everything that Gerald had felt in his heart and had seen in his mind unfolded and came to pass. As the saying goes, where God guides, God provides!

Do you allow God the opportunity to speak to you in the same way He spoke to Gerald's heart?

Don't Make Prayer a Monologue

Prayer is not simply a monologue—a one-way conversation. Rather, it is to be a dialogue between us and God. Prayer is a special time that consists not only of our speaking to God, but also of His speaking to us! We may not always hear or sense a message from Him, but we should at least give Him the opportunity to communicate to us by being open to the leading of His Spirit and quieting ourselves to hear His voice.

There are many different ways that God can speak to us. It's a good idea to keep your Bible with you when you pray, because there may be times when He will lead you to a specific passage of Scripture that is just what you need to calm you, direct you, clarify an issue, or confirm something that you have been feeling in your heart.

Another way the Lord may speak to us is through impressions in our hearts. In my thirty-plus years in ministry, I have seldom heard an audible voice telling me what to do or giving me a revelation. That's not to say that God doesn't speak in that way, but in my experience, He has spoken mostly in other, more subtle ways. It is usually in that still, small voice. (See 1 Kings 19:12.)

> TYPICALLY, THE WAY I KNOW THE VOICE AND SPIRIT OF GOD IS BY AN IMPRESSION THAT I SENSE IN MY HEART OR MIND. A SCRIPTURE WILL COME TO MIND OR WILL "HIT ME" AS I'M READING THE WORD.

If God spoke audibly all the time, it would certainly make our decisions a whole lot easier, wouldn't it? Typically, however, the way I know the voice and Spirit of God is by an impression that I sense in my heart or mind. A Scripture will come to mind or will "hit me" as I'm reading the Word. When this happens, the written Word—the *logos*—is becoming the living Word—the *rhema*. That is what's happening when the words written on the pages come out of the book and into your heart! They come to life and become real to you in one of those "aha" moments. This is also part of the process of taking ownership of the promises of God. We suddenly realize that while His promises were written for all people and for all time, they were also written for us, personally, for this very moment!

Another way to discern the mind of God for your life is if you feel confusion begin to fall away and be replaced by a sense of peace and clarity regarding the direction that you should take. You just feel it in your "knower."

Conviction versus Condemnation

In 1 John 3:21–22, we read, *"Beloved, if our heart condemn us not, then, we have confidence toward God. And whatsoever we ask, we receive of him, because we keep his commandments, and do those things that are pleasing in his sight."* I want to talk about the difference between conviction and condemnation. We hear many teachings that warn us about being prideful, and we've seen the destruction that a prideful spirit can leave in its wake.

To tell you the truth, though, I've seen more destruction in the lives of individuals due to low self-esteem and unfounded self-condemnation than from blatant pride and arrogance. Excessive self-condemnation can keep people from feeling worthy to approach God or expecting great things in their lives, even though they're promised these things in the Bible. It makes them afraid and intimidated to step into the destinies that God has promised them in His Word. And it will hinder any dreams from becoming reality.

To prevent this from happening in our lives, let's clarify the distinction between conviction and condemnation, two possible feelings that can come during prayer.

Conviction Is Clear and Specific

Conviction comes from the Lord. It is that still, small voice that guides us and keeps us on the correct path. If we say or do something hurtful or wrong, we immediately feel a sting in our hearts. We know exactly what we said or did; and we know exactly what we need to do to make it right. You know that feeling, just as I do. If we are grouchy and speak sharp words to our spouses or friends, we quickly realize that this isn't acceptable to the

> WITHHOLDING FORGIVENESS ISN'T WORTH LOSING SLEEP OVER! BITE YOUR TONGUE, PUT AWAY YOUR PRIDE, AND MAKE IT RIGHT!

Lord. We need to be quick to apologize to them and to God, and to make it right. Right?

The Bible exhorts us, *"Let not the sun go down upon your wrath"* (Ephesians 4:26). The apostle Paul was telling us to settle things and make things right at the end of each day before going to sleep. No one likes to toss and turn all night, kept awake by the memory of an argument or a guilty conscience. Withholding forgiveness isn't worth losing sleep over! Bite your tongue, put away your pride, and make it right! Work toward having a heart that is quick to repent—it makes life much easier!

Again, conviction brings clear feelings and specific direction as to what you have done wrong and what you must do to correct it. Conviction springs from an understanding of God's Word and what it has to say about how to live in God-honoring ways.

Condemnation Is Vague and Dark

Condemnation, on the other hand, is vague and lays a sense of heaviness on us. We're not really sure what we did wrong, but we're sure we must have done something! We feel a heavy, dark cloud of condemnation hanging over us, shadowing our minds. Conviction comes from the Lord to guide us; condemnation comes from the enemy to rob us of our joy, to steal blessings from our futures, and ultimately to defeat us.

Do you remember the character named Pig-Pen from the Charlie Brown cartoon strip by Charles Schulz? He had a cloud of dirt and dust that followed him wherever he went. That's how I see the cloud of condemnation—a vague cloud that comes straight from the pit of hell and pursues us wherever we go.

Of course, the enemy is also a master at bringing up genuine failures from our pasts and using them to condemn us. He does this by making us doubt God's mercy and forgiveness. Listen: if we repent, we receive God's forgiveness; whatever we did is under the blood of Jesus, never to be brought against us again! God forgives and then forgets. He even said, *"I will be merciful to* [your] *unrighteousness, and* [your] *sins and* [your] *iniquities will I remember no more"* (Hebrews 8:12).

"The Accuser of Our Brethren"

Revelation 12:10 calls the devil *"the accuser of our brethren."* The name of his game is to accuse God's children of all kinds of things in order to make us feel like we will never measure up and that God is frowning at us all the time. Satan loves to lay guilt trips on us, accusing us of being weak, stupid, unworthy, and so forth.

The first step to getting rid of condemnation is recognizing where it's coming from—the devil. God would never speak to His children with condemning accusations. Instead, He convicts us about specific, sinful words, actions, thoughts, and habits in order to move us to higher levels and to make us more like Him. Always remember: God is never pointing a finger of accusation at you. He's reaching out a hand to help you.

Discerning God's Mind and Voice Is an Ongoing Journey

Our relationships with God are alive and dynamic, so they're continually developing and growing. In a human relationship, the more time two people spend together, the more they know how the other person thinks and reacts, what he likes and dislikes, and so forth. And so it is with God—the more time we spend with Him, the better we know Him!

I like to tell this story about an elderly married couple. They had been together through thick and thin for more than fifty years. As the wife was preparing dinner one night, she came around the corner into the living room and asked her husband, "Now, which one of us is it who doesn't like broccoli?" Have you ever observed a husband and wife who have been together for so long that they begin to think alike, act alike, and even look alike? Quite literally, the two become one! That seems funny, but it's true!

And that's exactly what starts to happen to us the longer we know the Lord and the more time we spend with Him in prayer and reading His Word. A transformation takes place in our thinking—our carnal, limited ways of thinking are transformed into God's supernaturally wise way of thinking. His thoughts become our thoughts. His vision becomes our vision. His faith, peace, and confidence become ours. His limitless, eternal mind breaks open our limited, small mind-sets. The two become one as we become consumed with Him and reflect His image more closely.

> HIS THOUGHTS BECOME OUR THOUGHTS. HIS VISION BECOMES OUR VISION. HIS FAITH, PEACE, AND CONFIDENCE BECOME OURS.

Don't Allow Prayer to Become a Stagnant Ritual

During the course of our ministry, Larry and I have always held various types of prayer meetings. We've had daily prayer meetings at 6:00 a.m. so that men and women could join together in prayer before going to work. We've had hour-long prayer meetings before every service on Sunday mornings and Wednesday evenings. And many times, we have organized all-night prayer and intercession meetings. At these meetings in particular, it is easy to allow our minds to wander rather than focus on our prayers. We may be speaking words with our lips, but our minds are somewhere else! We may be making a grocery list, checking items off a to-do list, imagining how nice it would be to go to sleep, planning our family vacation, trying to figure out how to solve the problems that we ought to be praying about, and so forth. No doubt, we've all been guilty of doing this at some point!

One prayer meeting in particular comes to mind. All of the participants were kneeling down in front of metal folding chairs as they prayed for God to pour out His Spirit and interceded for souls. I glanced over to see a man on his knees praying out loud for God to move. On the floor next to his chair, his three-year-old son was playing quietly with a few toys. I looked back at the man and realized that while his lips were moving and words were coming out of them, his mind was occupied with another task. He was busily coloring pictures in his son's coloring book! This struck me as both funny and ridiculous. If we're going to put in the time and effort to pray, let's get focused and accomplish some serious things! Let's touch the heart of God with our sincerity!

Our Prayers Can Touch the Heart of God and Move the Hand of God

When our prayers touch the heart of God, they move the hand of God. But prayer should not consist of our trying to convince Him how terrible and pitiful our situations are and begging Him to have mercy and help us. The Bible tells us that *"without faith it is impossible to please God, because anyone who comes to him must believe that he exists and that he rewards those who earnestly seek him"* (Hebrews 11:6 NIV). Faith is nothing more than taking God at His word.

> GOD LOVES IT WHEN WE STRETCH OUR FAITH AND PUT FAITH-DEMANDS ON HIS PROMISES.

I know that when we come before Him full of faith, hope, and confidence, it pleases Him. It honors Him when we believe in His promises more than we believe what our circumstances indicate. It exalts Him when we are convinced that God is stronger than our enemy. It pleases Him when we take the time to read the Word that He has given us, and when we come before Him with boldness and confidence to stake our claims on what He has promised to us. He loves it when we stretch our faith and put faith-demands on His promises. When we take hold of His promises, we're not being disrespectful or presumptuous. Rather, we're acting in the way He has directed us to! *"Let us then approach the throne of grace with confidence, so that we may receive mercy and find grace to help us in our time of need"* (Hebrews 4:16 NIV). This is how we touch the heart of God and move the hand of God.

Our Words Create Something Positive or Negative

When you pray, briefly tell the Lord what needs you have and what issues you are facing. Psalm 55:22 says, *"Cast your cares on the LORD and he will sustain you"* (NIV). Then, spend the majority of your time thanking Him for the answers and speaking the Word and His promises over those needs and issues. Work the Word. Call in the blessings. Speak the solutions. Frame your world with the Word. When we speak God's Word, we are literally releasing it and bringing it into existence!

Remember, when God created the universe, He didn't pull out a hammer and chisel to build it. He *spoke* it into existence! He spoke, and the world was formed, along with everything in it! That same creative force is within you and me because He lives within us and we're made in His image! When we speak, we create—good or bad, positive or negative. That's why it's critical that we guard what we say. The Lord has entrusted us with an incredible force—the power to literally create our world with our words.

So, let's make a habit of praying, speaking, and responding to every challenge with the promises in God's Word. This will probably require a mindset adjustment. Rather than focusing on our problems, we should focus on our solutions. Instead of being consumed with our challenges, we should become consumed with God's promises. Instead of spending our time telling God how big our problems are, we should be telling our problems how big our God is!

From glory to glory, He's changing us! And believe me when I tell you that God loves you, and you are worthy of all the blessings He wants to pour on you. So, get ready!

Prayer and Promise Principles

- Prayer is not meant to be a monologue but rather a dynamic dialogue between us and our heavenly Father.

- When we remain open to the guidance of God's Holy Spirit, we allow Him to communicate with us, whether through a specific passage of Scripture, an impression in our hearts, a newfound sense of clarity, or another avenue.

- Conviction from the Lord brings a clear comprehension of what you have done wrong and what is necessary in order to correct it; condemnation is a vague sense of heaviness that comes from the enemy.

- Frame your world with the Word by speaking out the promises of God!

- Rather than telling God how big our problems are, let's tell our problems how big our God is! Rather than focusing on our problems, let's focus on God's solutions!

- Work the Word! Speak out God's promises! Call in God's blessings!

Chapter Six

PRIORITIZING PRAYER IN A BUSY SCHEDULE

There is absolutely no experience in life that could compare to the experience of spending focused, uninterrupted time with the Lord in worship, praise, and prayer. The incredible opportunity and privilege that we each have to develop a deep, genuine relationship with God Almighty should never be taken for granted. It's been said that the greatest expression of genuine love is time spent with a person, and this certainly applies to our relationships with the Lord. The people and things we most value are evident in how we spend our time. A genuine, intimate relationship with the Lord is the basis for strong faith, peace, and joy in our spiritual and emotional lives. It is also the basis for every breakthrough and all lasting success in our lives.

Ideally, we would go into our "prayer closet" each morning and spend an entire, uninterrupted hour in prayer. But in reality, most people find it extremely difficult to set aside an hour for prayer on a daily basis. This doesn't mean, however, that they can't have fruitful prayer lives that bring them closer and closer to the heart of God. My goal is to teach you how to fit powerful prayers with amazing results into your everyday life. Let's set some goals for our prayer lives that are more feasible and realistic, given our busy schedules.

Ideal Prayer Life versus Real Prayer Life

We all desire to know God more deeply and to see the demonstration of His power, but many of us feel that we lack the time to pray adequately

"SOMEWHERE BETWEEN WHAT WE CAN AND CANNOT DO, WE DO NOTHING." UNFORTUNATELY, THIS STATEMENT APPLIES TO THE PRAYER LIVES OF MANY OF US. BUT THAT DOESN'T HAVE TO BE THE CASE!

in order to see these desires fulfilled. In a perfect world, we could all spend countless hours before the Lord, worshipping, praying, and interceding.

In the real world, however, we have babies to feed, children to chauffeur to soccer practice, dishes to wash, meals to prepare, church functions to attend, paychecks to earn…the list goes on. Sleep is continually calling us to catch up, and there's barely enough time to rest and relax, let alone do something we want to do for our own enjoyment. We usually end up shifting prayer to last place on our to-do lists, not because we want to, but because of the ever-increasing demands that crowd our schedules and consume our time. Despite our good intentions, at the end of the day, we fall into bed and try to forget the feelings of guilt we feel because we never found the time to pray. There is a saying that insightfully points out, "Somewhere between what we can and cannot do, we do nothing." Unfortunately, this statement applies to the prayer lives of many of us. But that doesn't have to be the case!

Start Where You Are and Do What You Can

I have always tried to be a person of prayer. By the grace of God, I have seen and experienced amazing miracles in my life, the lives of my family members, and the lives of many others that were answers to prayer. Commitment to my prayer life has allowed me to experience the deep, miraculous realms of answered prayer. But, to be honest with you, I face the same time constraints and scheduling issues of a busy, hectic life as you probably do. The reality of my prayer life is this: as often as I can, I take an hour to engage in diligent, powerful prayer; if time does not permit this, I pray on the go! Either way, prayer is a regular part of my daily existence, and as a result, God has a part in every aspect of my life.

My children—all adults now—are also powerful people of prayer, and most of their "prayer training" took place in the car on the way to school every morning. You know that old saying, "Necessity is the mother of invention"? Well, this mother says, "Life in the fast lane is the mother of innovation." We've got to do the best we can with whatever we've got!

I have realized not only that effective prayer doesn't require buckets of tears or weeping and wailing, but also that it doesn't require hours and hours of endless travailing before God. I'm going to teach you how to streamline your prayers and gain immediate access to the Lord. We'll discover how to achieve optimal results without hours of effort on our parts. We can incorporate prayer into our busy lives, accomplishing our own tasks and simultaneously following the apostle Paul's exhortation to *"pray without ceasing"* (1 Thessalonians 5:17).

The Bible talks about many different types of prayer, as well as the different times when we are to pray. I will highlight a few of these; the rest you can explore on your own. There are too many types of prayer to even mention here, and to define each of them in detail would require volumes! My objective is to not get bogged down with complex and convoluted details but rather to keep our discussion simple, powerful, and capable of producing results.

The Appointed Hour of Prayer

The Word talks repeatedly about the appointed hour of prayer. This is the designated time, first thing in the morning, when we set aside the affairs and duties of life and focus completely on the Lord and His Word through prayer. This is the time when we make a determined effort to communicate and connect with Him and with all of His promises. We worship Him, engage in spiritual warfare, bind the power of the enemy, and release the power of God.

The following Scriptures are examples of this type of prayer in the Bible:

They [Hannah, the mother of Samuel, and her husband, Elkanah] *rose up in the morning early, and worshipped before the* LORD.
(1 Samuel 1:19)

My voice shalt thou hear in the morning, O LORD; in the morning will I direct my prayer unto thee, and will look up. (Psalm 5:3)

I will sing of thy power; yea, I will sing aloud of thy mercy in the morning: for thou hast been my defence and refuge in the day of my trouble. (Psalm 59:16)

O God, thou art my God; early will I seek thee. (Psalm 63:1)

Very early in the morning, when it was still dark, Jesus got up, left the house and went off to a solitary place, where he prayed. (Mark 1:35 NIV)

OUR APPOINTED HOUR AND PLACE CAN BE IN OUR PRAYER CLOSETS, OUR PRAYER CARS, OR OUR PRAYER SHOWERS!

Now, if we were perfect people in a perfect world, we would seclude ourselves and pray for at least one uninterrupted hour every morning. For those of us who are not at all perfect and are not living in a perfect world—and that's most of us—our appointed hour and place can be in our prayer closets, our prayer cars, or our prayer showers! Whether you can spend an entire hour in prayer or can squeeze in only ten or twenty minutes, what counts is your sincerity. Start where you are and do what you can.

First and Final Daily Appointments with the Lord

Always try to make your first and last appointments of the day with the Lord. As soon as you wake up in the morning, allow His Spirit to instill in you a sense of expectancy and a faith for the plans He has in store for you that day. Let Him pour into your mind and spirit His joy, confidence, strength, wisdom, and insight to equip you to serve Him and others. Then, at the end of the day, just before you go to sleep, let His Spirit fill you with peace, calm, hope, and rest.

The psalmist said, *"Evening, and morning, and at noon, will I pray, and cry aloud: and he shall hear my voice"* (Psalm 55:17). Our God is alert and attentive to hear our heartfelt prayers, and He is actively working to bring them to pass! When we start and end our days with the Lord, we can't help but walk in victory throughout the entire day!

Praying on the Go

In my experience, fifteen to twenty minutes of "prayer on the go" is better than an hour of "intended to, but actually never got to" prayer! Certainly, all of us can improve our diligence and commitment to regular prayer, but for now, let's take it in bite-sized pieces. I am convinced that as we begin to see the changes that take place, the burdens that are removed, and the miracles that are released, we will increase the amount of time we spend in prayer. The truth is that our God can accomplish more during five minutes of prayer than we can accomplish through fifty hours of labor! Think of your prayer time not as an activity that depletes your time and efforts but as an activity that supernaturally enhances your time and multiplies your efforts!

I like to illustrate this concept with the following analogy. You have probably seen or even used a moving walkway in an airport, subway station, or a large mall. These walkways are convenient in airports, particularly if you're running late for your flight. As you step on and walk at a normal pace, they carry you along at an increased speed so that with every step, you cover much more ground than you would by simply walking on solid ground.

This is how I envision our lives when we pray things through. God puts His super to our natural to turbocharge, streamline, and multiply all of our labors, efforts, and time. Remember, prayer is a divine exchange—we trade our natural strengths, abilities, and effectiveness for His limitless power, equipping, help, and resources! As we invest our time in prayer, He multiplies our time back to us. Many times in my own busy life, the Lord has multiplied my time in many ways. For instance, I will be at the grocery store or at the airport, and there will be no lines to wait in. From the smallest ways to the largest ways, He will always multiply and give back whatever we invest! He always makes sure that it is a good trade!

Praying at the Speed of Life

I don't know anyone who is not constantly pressed for time. If we're going to fit prayer into our daily schedules, we might need to use a little innovation and creativity. We have to learn to pray at the speed of life! So...

How about making rush hour your prayer hour? Pray in the car on your way to work or when driving your children to school! As long as you're driving, why not drive the enemy right out of your life?

- When you're working out, work the Word of God over your future!

- Make the time that you shower the time you empower!

- While putting on your makeup, put on the mind of Christ!

- As you get dressed, clothe your spirit with the Word of God!

- As you're doing housework, do your faith declarations!

- While you're cutting your lawn, you might as well cut off the enemy's power in your life!

- When you're taking a power walk, have some power talk. Declare that every plan that the enemy has for you, your family, and your friends is canceled!

- As you launder or iron clothes for your family members, cover their minds, spirits, and bodies with the protection of God and His angels! Bind the enemy's influence over them!

- While you are folding the laundry, get fired up and break every spirit of lack and insufficiency over your finances and release every blessing of increase, abundance, and overflow!

- As the events of your day unfold, frame your world with the Word of God! You'll be spending this time doing various tasks anyway, so why not multitask and multiply your efforts?

Praying while You Sleep

Did you know that we can pray while we're sleeping? No, I'm not giving you an excuse to hit the snooze button, fall back to sleep, and dream that you're praying (something many of us have done more than once). Nor am I talking about some strange, cosmic dream state.

What I mean is that we may ask the Lord to give us direction and to clarify His will for us during our sleep. I do this a lot myself, often when I'm trying to figure something out or make an important decision, or if I'm feeling stuck in my search for a solution and in need of fresh inspiration.

The last thing I do at night is ask the Lord to orchestrate my thoughts during my sleep and to give me direction during the night.

WE MAY ASK THE LORD TO GIVE US DIRECTION AND TO CLARIFY HIS WILL FOR US DURING OUR SLEEP.

Now, let me give you a little warning about this. We need to keep in mind that not every dream comes from the Lord. Hear me and trust me on this! Many a confused and frightened soul have I had to redirect and reassure because of some absurd, random dream. Not every strange dream that you have is God telling you to do some wild and crazy thing! Most dreams are no more than that: dreams—bizarre, meaningless, inconsequential dreams that are often the results of late-night pizza fests or scary movies! They may also be the subconscious illustrations of some unresolved emotional conflicts. Who knows where our wacky dreams come from? And who really cares? Don't place too much weight on the "meanings" of your nightly dreams.

While it's important to avoid getting caught up in interpreting and analyzing our dreams, it's also true that even while we're dreaming, the Lord can settle our thoughts, direct our paths, and illuminate His plans for us. Remember the wise old saying that our mothers used to tell us when we were troubled about something? They said, "Just sleep on it. You'll know what to do in the morning." Well, that wise old saying sums up what happens when the Lord takes our times of slumber as opportunities to move on our behalf. Again, I have made a habit of asking the Lord in prayer to direct my thoughts as I sleep. Then, when I wake up in the morning, I take a few minutes to pay attention to the thoughts in my head. During this time, it's not uncommon for new or important ideas to come to me, for solutions to problems to formulate in my mind, for scattered thoughts to coalesce in a logical way, or for wisdom I've been seeking to finally arrive. At other times, I'll find myself suddenly wide awake in the middle of the night, usually at three o'clock sharp, roused by a complete plan or idea.

I have learned to pay attention during these times and to write down whatever I am feeling or thinking. Again, let me emphasize that not every one of these occurrences is necessarily a revelation from the Lord. Over

THE LORD WANTS US TO KNOW AND BE ABLE TO RECOGNIZE HIS VOICE, HIS SPIRIT, AND HIS DIRECTION. HE WILL FIND WAYS TO CONFIRM THAT WE'RE ON THE RIGHT TRACK.

time, however, we develop discernment as our experiences confirm what we have thought or seen during our sleep. The Lord wants us to know and be able to recognize His voice, His Spirit, and His direction. He will find ways to confirm that we're on the right track. He desires to commune with us even more than we desire to commune with Him! Never make an important life decision based on a dream without having other confirmations to back it up. When the Lord is involved in our dreams, there's just something that rings true and lines up to clarify each issue we face. Praying for God's involvement in your dream life and paying attention to divine direction when you wake up in the morning is just another way to get in the habit of making your first and final daily appointments with your heavenly Father.

Our Ultimate Goal: Praying Continually

First Thessalonians 5:16–18 exhorts us, *"Be joyful always; pray continually, give thanks in all circumstances, for this is God's will for you in Christ Jesus"* (NIV). To *"pray continually"* (*"without ceasing"* KJV) does not mean that we continually mumble prayers aloud all day. Rather, it means that we are in a constant state of prayer within our minds and hearts. Throughout the entire day, in every situation we're involved in, we maintain an awareness of God's presence and ask quietly for His help, direction, and equipping. Remaining open to His voice and leading, we feel the presence and direction of God. We keep ourselves in a continual spirit of gratitude toward Him. With God's passion infusing our lives and His Spirit indwelling our spirits, we converse with Him during the course of each day. We give the Lord the ongoing opportunity to lead us, direct us, and speak to us. If we encounter a challenge, we bring it to the Lord and conquer it with His Word. Over time, this state of constant prayerfulness becomes as natural as breathing.

Principles to Practice regardless of Your Prayer Pattern

Let's not be like the fictitious family who planned a road trip but loaded so much baggage in their car that they had to remove the engine to make room for even more stuff! That's a great picture of what we don't want to happen in our spiritual lives. Let's be sure that we don't end up packing so much baggage into our lives that we take out the engine—the equipping power of God—to make room for more stuff! With the jam-packed lives many of us lead, we definitely need God's supernatural help to empower our natural efforts.

Before you focus on your to-do list for the day, focus on your equipping list—the Lord's presence and His promises. Each morning before rushing into your day, rush into the presence of God. Concentrate on God's supply list, which provides above and beyond what we need to meet the challenges and demands of each day.

On many mornings, we hit the snooze button five or six times, then fly out of bed, grab a granola bar, and off we go, never giving as much as one thought to God, let alone a prayer. All the tasks and the cares of the day start to pile up so quickly that we often forget to take the time to focus on how big, how powerful, how available our God is. We end up struggling through the day and facing the toils of life with our own limited strength and with our own limited abilities and resources instead of drawing from the divine Source of infinite power, wisdom, and strength. Before we face the big problems in the world, we need to equip ourselves with the even bigger promises that are found in the Word of God. Instead of telling God how big our problems are, let's tell our problems how big our God is!

Again, let's not look at prayer as one more item on our to-do lists. Instead, let's look at prayer as a way of casting our cares on God, whose to-do list is long enough to accommodate every need of every person on the face of the earth. Remember, prayer is where we trade in our shortcomings for God's abundant equipping; where we connect His super to our natural. It's a divine exchange. We all lead busy, hectic lives, but let's not shortchange ourselves by leaving out the most important component of our success.

PRAYER AND PROMISE PRINCIPLES

- A busy schedule and a fruitful prayer life are not mutually exclusive, contrary to popular opinion.
- Effective prayer doesn't require buckets of tears or hours of weeping and wailing, so we can incorporate prayer in even the busiest of lives.
- Regardless of our schedules, we should start every day by worshipping God and calling on His promises in prayer.
- We should also finish each day with a time of communion with the Lord, during which He will fill us with peace, calm, hope, and rest.
- Praying on the go is preferable to not praying at all.
- Our ultimate goal is to pray without ceasing—being engaged in ongoing communication with our heavenly Father.
- Prayer isn't just another item on our to-do lists; it's a privilege that empowers us to accomplish everything on those lists!

Chapter Seven

OUR RIGHT TO RECEIVE GOD'S BLESSINGS

S everal years ago, a friend of ours was given the opportunity to meet and interview a gentleman who was one of the richest, most influential men in the world at that time. He was also one of the kindest, happiest, and most contented people our friend had ever met. This gentleman lived in a multimillion-dollar mansion on a massive estate at the base of the Swiss Alps. His windows offered spectacular views of the mountains.

As our friend and this gentleman sat together on the terrace gazing at this amazing view, our friend asked, "How is it that you are so successful in life? Tell me the main keys to your ongoing accomplishments and wealth."

The Swiss gentleman replied, "Well, you probably wouldn't believe me if I told you."

Our friend said, "Please, I really want to know what the foundations to your success are."

So, he agreed to explain the foundation upon which his successes had been built. He said, "Every morning, there is something I do as soon as I get up, before I meet with any businesspeople, staff, and even my wife or family. The first thing I do is to get a big cup of coffee, go out on my terrace, and just sit and fellowship with the Lord. I worship Him and bask in His presence. I express my love to Him, and I enjoy His love toward me. I gaze out over the Swiss Alps, which are so incredibly magnificent, and I think about how God, with just one swipe of His finger, created all of those enormous, beautiful mountains. I focus my thoughts on how big our God is to have so easily created these peaks. I think about the creative genius that is within the mind of God to have designed such beauty. I take pleasure in realizing that the Lord created this amazing world for His children to enjoy. I realize and focus on the fact that all of this world was created by and belongs to God Almighty, and that it is our Father's good pleasure to give His children the kingdom. It is God's will to put His children into positions of high influence, authority, power, and wealth.

"I then let it sink into my spirit that God, our Father, is in charge of everything that takes place in this world. I accept the privilege and the responsibility that God has given us each individual talents and gifting, with which we are entrusted to make the world a better place. Before I even speak one word, I let all of that sink into my spirit.

"Then I begin to pray and ask the Lord, 'Father, show me what You are doing in the world today and how You want me to be a part of that.' Then I just let Him begin to speak to me, direct me, and give me insight into my day. I allow God the time to inspire me with ideas, concepts, and insights.

"Sometimes, God will speak to me to call a certain person, and, sure enough, a world-shaking deal will come about out of that. Or, maybe the Lord will check me in my spirit about a deal or a person I need to steer clear of. Other times, God will drop a plan, an idea, an invention, or an investment opportunity into my mind that will lead to huge financial breakthroughs. God will also speak to me about the many areas that I need to sow into financially. As much as He speaks to me about how to *make* money, He speaks to me about how to *give* that money away!

> THE MORE I GIVE AWAY, THE MORE GOD GIVES BACK TO ME. I HAVE MADE THE PRIORITY OF MY LIFE NOT ABOUT WORKING TO LIVE BUT ABOUT WORKING TO GIVE.

"Then, once I have heard the voice of God, I quickly act on those directions! A large part of the direction that I receive from the Lord is about where to sow and give my finances away. The more I give away, the more God gives back to me. I have made the priority of my life not about working to *live* but about working to *give*. I am simply a steward of what the Lord puts in my hands and though my hands. My desire and goal is to see how much one man can give away in a lifetime!"

And that is the foundation to all of this man's outstanding success and abundant wealth, influence, and contentment. All of us would do well to put these principles into practice, for they've been proven with incredible results by more people than just this Swiss gentleman.

Blessed to Be a Blessing

I absolutely believe that God has ordained each and every one of us to be a person of powerful, positive influence with many great successes and significant amounts of wealth and resources to pour into the work of God. When we make up our minds to be conduits of God's blessings, He will make certain to get them to us and through us! I am convinced that our God wants to bless us greatly so that we can be great blessings.

Life is God's gift to us, and it can also be our gift to Him when we surrender our lives to Him and live for His glory. It's time for us to start thinking like the Swiss businessman. Let's take the limits off of our small-minded human thinking! Our God is a big God; He is a supremely good, loving, kind, and generous God. He has big plans for the life of every one of us, and we need to develop God-sized visions for our lives in order to fulfill those plans. This way, we can tap into all that He is and all that He has made available to us!

God's mercy, grace, and help are inexhaustible. His love for us is never-ending. His equipping and resources are limitless. All we have to do is take the time and make the effort to come to Him and tap into His never-ending supply!

Countless Promises Await You

Changing your attitude toward prayer and making it a top priority in your life will drastically change the course of your every day. More than that—it will change your whole life! We need to face life with the confidence that God intends for us to walk in His authority and dominion. He doesn't want us living under the circumstances of life; He wants us to live above them! We are more than conquerors, as Paul proclaimed in Romans 8:37.

No matter what comes our way, nothing can separate us from the promises and love of God—*"neither death, nor life, nor angels, nor principalities, nor powers, nor things present, nor things to come, nor height, nor depth, nor any other creature"* (verses 38–39). We all want the promises of God to be manifested in our lives. We all want the good things of God for ourselves, our families, our communities, our nations, and our world. We want to see those promises operating full-time and in every area! Taking personal ownership of God's Word and then praying it through is how we make that divine connection and transact that divine exchange.

But we need to *ask* for the promises that are ours by right, and we do this by calling on God in prayer. Psalm 145:18–19 gives us this assurance: *"The LORD is near to all who call on him, to all who call on him in truth. He fulfills the desires of those who fear him; he hears their cry and saves them"* (NIV). In Ephesians 6:18, we are instructed to *"pray in the Spirit on all occasions with all kinds of prayers and requests"* (NIV). Philippians 4:4 is a reminder to *"rejoice in the Lord always. I will say it again: Rejoice!"* (NIV). And verses 6–7 tell us, *"Do not be anxious about anything, but in everything, by prayer and petition, with thanksgiving, present your requests to God. And the peace of God, which transcends all understanding, will guard your hearts and your minds in Christ Jesus"* (NIV).

Simply put: don't worry about anything, but pray about everything; cast your cares upon Jesus, and the peace of God will fill your heart, mind, and life.

Again, Ephesians 6:18 tells us to *"pray in the Spirit on all occasions with all kinds of prayers and requests"* (NIV). Every request and all manner of needs— God wants to hear them! Thank God that we can come to Him and call upon Him at any moment and with any need. No matter who we are, He will hear us and help us!

A Biblical Example of Seizing God's Promises by Faith

In the book of Romans, Paul talked about the stance of faith that Abraham and Sarah had to take in order to receive God's promise of a child. Think about how crazy that promise must have seemed in the natural to them and to everyone else! Both Abraham and Sarah were well past the normal childbearing years. But they reached out in faith, grabbed God's promise, and received their miracle child. This was a case of being literally pregnant with the promise! Abraham,

> *without weakening in his faith…faced the fact that his body was as good as dead—since he was about a hundred years old—and that Sarah's womb was also dead. Yet he did not waver through unbelief regarding the promise of God, but was strengthened in his faith and gave glory to God, being fully persuaded that God had power to do what he had promised.*
>
> (Romans 4:19–21 NIV)

The example of these heroes of the faith, our ancestors Abraham and Sarah, should give us all great hope as we stand in faith for our own miracles.

One reason that we may struggle to exhibit the faith of Abraham and Sarah is that this kind of faith is not a natural action—it's a supernatural one because it believes in supernatural things. And Abraham and Sarah were not so different from you and me. Think about it: just like we do, they had to choose to believe what God had spoken to them. Romans 4:18 tells us that Abraham *"against hope believed in hope"*; in other words, although the odds were against him, and although common sense contradicted him completely, he chose to believe God.

Abraham and Sarah chose to believe, *"being fully persuaded that, what [God] had promised, he was able also to perform"* (Romans 4:21). And choosing to believe is not a one-time deal. We have to make continual choices—day after day, week after week, and year after year—that propel us down the paths of our destinies. We must keep asserting and exercising our faith in God's promises. This won't always be easy, especially when the odds are against you and when common sense tells you something different. But each time that you witness God's miraculous intervention on your behalf, it becomes easier to believe for even greater miracles from Him.

ONE REASON THAT WE MAY STRUGGLE TO EXHIBIT THE FAITH OF ABRAHAM AND SARAH IS THAT THIS KIND OF FAITH IS NOT A NATURAL ACTION—IT'S A SUPERNATURAL ONE BECAUSE IT BELIEVES IN SUPERNATURAL THINGS.

What an endlessly exciting journey we're on! We are never limited to our own human abilities, strengths, or resources. Expect the unexpected! With our God, all things are possible! (See Matthew 19:26; Mark 10:27.)

It's Your Time

It's time for you to live at a new level of dominion and authority. It's time for you to be filled with continual joy, excitement, and expectation! It's time for you to see each and every blessing released into your life! It's time for you become the lender and not the borrower! It's time for you and your family to live in divine health! It's time for you to possess every one of the eight thousand promises of God that have your name on them!

My friend, say it out loud right now: "It's my time!" Okay, this time, shout it out: "IT'S MY TIME!" That's how you begin to take ownership of the promises of God!

PRAYER AND PROMISE PRINCIPLES

- When we make up our minds to be conduits of God's blessings, He will make certain to get them to us and through us! God wants to bless us greatly so that we can be great blessings.

- Life is God's gift to us, and it can also be our gift to Him when we surrender our lives to Him and live for His glory.

- God's mercy, grace, and help are inexhaustible. His equipping and resources are limitless. All we have to do is tap into His never-ending supply!

- We need to face life with the confidence that God intends for us to walk in His authority and dominion. Through Him, we are more than conquerors!

- No matter who we are, God will hear us and help us! He is ready, willing, and able to help us at any moment and in all circumstances.

- Great faith is not a natural action—it's a supernatural one, because it believes in supernatural things.

- Choosing to believe for God's promises to become realities in our lives is not a one-time deal; it's something we must do on a daily basis.

- *Now* is your time to possess the promises of God!

POSSESSING THE PROMISES OF GOD THROUGH PRAYER

Chapter Eight

Step One: Trust the Promise Maker

The first step in seeing our prayers answered is to realize that our God is good, kind, and loving. He is ready, willing, and able to help us and to meet our needs.

To understand why we can trust God to help us, let's consider part of the gospel account of an angel bringing some important news to the future parents of John the Baptist. *"The angel said unto [Zacharias], Fear not, Zacharias: for thy prayer is heard; and thy wife Elisabeth shall bear thee a son"* (Luke 1:13). The Greek word for *"prayer"* in this text is *deesis*, meaning "a petition, a supplication, an asking or entreating; a beseeching or wanting; a specific thing requested; and imploring God's help." The word *deesis* implies (1) our needs, (2) our inability to meet those needs on our own, and (3) God's willingness to hear, respond to, and meet those needs.

Deesis does not portray man appealing to a cold, indifferent God, but rather to a loving, compassionate Father who is eager and willing to help. We see a picture of man's extreme needs becoming God's extreme opportunities to hear and to help. He is ready, willing, and able to help us and to meet our needs!

In 1 Timothy 2:1, Paul wrote, *"I urge, then, first of all, that requests, prayers, intercession and thanksgiving be made for everyone"* (NIV). The type of prayer he was advocating with *"intercession"*—which is *enteuxis* in the original Greek, meaning a meeting or petition—implies intimacy, familiarity,

and heartfelt communion with our heavenly Father. The distinctive deno-
tations of this word include freedom of access, confidence, and holy intimacy, as we are invited to boldly approach the Lord to present our needs and
requests. Hebrews 4:16 says, *"Let us therefore come boldly unto the throne of
grace, that we may obtain mercy, and find grace to help in time of need."*

God Himself, through Jesus, *"in whom we have boldness and access with
confidence by the faith of him"* (Ephesians 3:12), has opened the door and allowed us total and complete access to His love, help, and resources.

Speaking about *enteuxis*, theologian William Barclay wrote, "Prayer
is nothing less than entering into the presence of the Almighty and receiving the resources of the Eternal."[3] We, as God's children, have been given
the tremendous privilege of free access to His
unlimited outpouring of power!

THE POWER OF GOD IS AN INCREDIBLE GIFT, AND HIS SECRETS ARE RARE TREASURES ENTRUSTED ONLY TO THOSE WHO ARE WILLING TO PRESS IN AND PURSUE HIM. TO KNOW HIM IS TO TRUST HIM.

It's All about Trust

In Jeremiah 33:3, the Lord offers an amazing opportunity to each of us. He says, *"Call
to me and I will answer you and tell you great
and unsearchable things you do not know"* (NIV).
The Word of God paints a consistent picture
of prayer as a relationship between us and the
Lord. His plan has always been to have an intimate, alive, and ongoing relationship with
every one of His children. It is out of this intimacy that great miracles are conceived and
then birthed in our lives.

The power of God is an incredible gift, and
His secrets are rare treasures entrusted only
to those who are willing to press in and pursue Him. To know Him is to trust Him. Psalm
37:5–6 says, *"Commit your way to the LORD; trust in him and he will do this:
he will make your righteousness shine like the dawn, the justice of your cause like*

[3] William Barclay, *New Testament Words* (Louisville, KY: Westminster John Knox Press, 2000), 86.

the noonday sun" (NIV), and Nahum 1:7 says, *"The Lord is good, a refuge in times of trouble. He cares for those who trust in him"* (NIV).

The more that we comprehend God's immense love for us, His attentiveness to hear our prayers, and His willingness to help us in every situation, the more faith and confidence rise up within us. In Psalm 66:18–20, the psalmist wrote, *"If I had cherished sin in my heart, the Lord would not have listened; but God has surely listened and heard my voice in prayer. Praise be to God, who has not rejected my prayer or withheld his love from me!"* (NIV). God does not withhold His love from us; He freely offers it, but we have to accept it. Understanding the Lord's love for us and His willingness to help us is the first step in taking ownership of the promises of God. This is how we begin literally possessing the promises of God.

A Sampling of Promises

There are a few Scriptures that I quote and hang on to every day (and many times a day). Three of my favorite promises from God's Word are these:

- *"God is not a man, that he should lie; neither the son of man, that he should repent* [change his mind]: *hath he said, and shall he not do it? or hath he spoken, and shall he not make it good?"* (Numbers 23:19). I like to put it like this: "If God didn't mean what He said, why didn't He say what He meant? And so, if He did say it and promise it, then He's going to make it happen!"

- *"So is my word that goes out from my mouth: it will not return to me empty, but will accomplish what I desire and achieve the purpose for which I sent it"* (Isaiah 55:11 NIV). God's Word cannot return to Him without accomplishing that which He sent it to do! When He speaks, He backs it up!

And then, I top those two Scriptures off with this one:

- *"I will hasten my word to perform it"* (Jeremiah 1:12). I really like the way this verse reads in the *New International Version:* "The Lord said to me, 'You have seen correctly, for I am watching to see that my word is fulfilled.'" Our God Himself is watching over His Word to make sure that it comes to pass in our lives!

Patience Is Often Needed

I am 100 percent convinced that the moment we pray about a situation, God turns the situation around. He sends our answer the moment we pray and ask. Sometimes, we see miraculous results immediately—oh, how we love those times! Sometimes, however, we have to continue praying through until we achieve our victory.

Daniel proved this very truth. In Daniel 9:20–21, he was praying for Jerusalem and asking God's forgiveness when the angel Gabriel finally arrived and said to him, *"Daniel, I have now come to give you insight and understanding. As soon as you began to pray, an answer was given, which I have come to tell you, for you are highly esteemed"* (verses 22–23 NIV).

Later, Daniel had a vision regarding a war, and he fasted and prayed for three weeks. When an angel finally arrived twenty-one days later, he told Daniel that God had sent him with the answer as soon as he had begun praying. However, the angel had needed to war with evil spirits in the heavens. He said to Daniel,

> Do not be afraid, Daniel. Since the first day that you set your mind to gain understanding and to humble yourself before your God, your words were heard, and I have come in response to them. But the prince of the Persian kingdom resisted me twenty-one days. Then Michael, one of the chief princes, came to help me, because I was detained there with the king of Persia.   (Daniel 10:12–13 NIV)

Just as Daniel had to continue interceding, sometimes we do, too. We've got to knock and keep on knocking. We have to keep pressing into the promises of God through prayer because there is a battle going on. We're tearing down strongholds and driving back the enemy, who usually puts up a nasty fight. He will never win, mind you, but he'll go down kicking and screaming.

Don't ever be intimidated by the enemy. The blood of Jesus has equipped you with more power than all the combined power in hell. Stand firmly and boldly on the promises, and the devil will back down. James 4:7–8 gives us this assurance: *"Submit yourselves, then, to God. Resist the devil, and he will flee from you. Come near to God and he will come near to you"* (NIV). What incredible power is at our disposal to bind the enemy and release the blessings! Our prayers will touch the heart and move the hand of our God. Don't ever give up on the Lord or on His promises, because He is watching over His Word to perform it!

Whenever we get anxious and feel discouraged because we aren't seeing the results we desire as fast as we desire them, we must "encourage ourselves" with the Word, just as David did in so many of the psalms he penned. Sometimes, we need to "stir ourselves up" like Paul encouraged Timothy to do with the gifts of God in 2 Timothy 1:6. These are the times when we choose to stop looking down at our circumstances and choose to look up at our Savior. We stop the downward spiral of fear and doubt, and we launch the upward ascent of faith, hope, and confidence. We override the circumstances of our lives with the promises of our God!

We calm the storms of life by standing firm on His promise that He is watching over His Word to bring it to pass. We're not just out there on our own, trying to make everything work out. There is no need for us to do so, for God is alert and actively involved in the affairs of our lives.

Believe in God's Promises of Blessing for You

Remember, there are so many promises of blessing in the Word just waiting for you to access them. Let's get in there together, find out what they are, and then activate them through prayer and declarations! Our words hold tremendous power to literally lift these promises out of the Book and create them into the realities of our lives.

Every morning, we can set our courses for the day. By making the choice to have positive, faith-filled attitudes and confessions, we will block the enemy's access to our lives. Again, Proverbs 4:23 instructs us, "Above all else, guard your heart, for it is the wellspring of life" (NIV). We each have to make a conscious choice—every day, and many times throughout the day—to remain focused on the promises of God. We all will face challenges, especially in the area of

> BY MAKING THE CHOICE TO HAVE POSITIVE, FAITH-FILLED ATTITUDES AND CONFESSIONS, WE WILL BLOCK THE ENEMY'S ACCESS TO OUR LIVES.

finances. As I have said over and over, challenges are not meant to overcome us; we are meant to overcome challenges.

Remember, one of the Lord's names is Jehovah Jireh, which means "God will provide." In our prayers, we're not begging Him to help us; we're simply entering into who He is and appropriating what He has already done for us. Rather than spending so much of our prayer time telling the Lord about our issues and needs, we should spend the majority of our time declaring the Word, proclaiming His promises, and releasing creative faith over the issues and needs in our lives. We are framing our world with the Word of God by exchanging our needs for His supply, our lack for His abundance, and our insufficiency for His riches!

Here are a few ways that we can set or alter the course of our days, as well as the course of our lives.

- Before we take a look at our bills and have a panic attack, let's take a look at God's promises of provision and have a praise session!

- When someone asks us how we're doing, let's resist laying out our list of troubles or grumbling, "Okay, I guess, under the circumstances...." Why not respond, "I'm great and getting greater! And on top of that, I'm highly favored by God! I don't live under the circumstances of the world. I live upon the circumstances of the Word"?

- If your children ask you to buy something that is beyond your budget, refrain from barking out, "We can't afford that! Do you think money grows on trees?" Tell them instead, "Let's pray together that the Lord will meet all of our needs and provide more than enough so that we can get that for you."

- If your money runs out before the month runs out, don't moan and groan and fuss and fret. Call upon Jehovah Jireh, your provider, and claim some of His promises of blessings!

- Instead of using so much time and energy talking about the negative, let's use that time and energy to speak out and create the positive!

- Rather than jumping into panic mode, jump into faith mode!

• Rather than magnifying our problems, let's magnify God's promises!

PRAYER AND PROMISE PRINCIPLES

• Through prayer, we're not appealing to a cold, indifferent God; we're communing with a loving, compassionate Father who is eager and willing to help.

• As God's children, we have been given the tremendous privilege of free access to His unlimited outpouring of power!

• God does not withhold His love from us; He freely offers it, but we have to accept it.

• The moment we pray about a situation, God turns it around, even if we have to pray with patience and persistence until we achieve our victory.

• We should spend the majority of our prayer time proclaiming God's promises and declaring His Word rather than rattling off long lists of needs and concerns.

Chapter Nine

STEP TWO:
KNOW THE PROMISES AVAILABLE

There are countless promises in the Bible with our names on them. Now we're going to discover how to get them out of the Bible and into our lives!

In John 8:32, Jesus said, *"You will know the truth, and the truth will set you free"* (NIV). We've already discussed how this Scripture does not say that the *truth* will set you free but that the *truth that you know* will set you free. In other words, we have to take personal ownership of the truths that are written in the Word in order for them to set us free or to have an effect on our lives.

In order to take ownership of the truth, we first have to know what the truth—the Word of God (see John 17:17)—promises to us. We can't lay claim to what we don't even know exists! If we had never read or heard that Jesus Christ lived and died to be our Savior, how would we be able to accept Him into our hearts? Paul raised this issue in the book of Romans.

"Everyone who calls on the name of the Lord will be saved." How, then, can they call on the one they have not believed in? And how can they believe in the one of whom they have not heard? And how can they hear without someone preaching to them? And how can they preach unless they are sent? As it is written, "How beautiful are the feet of those who bring good news!" But not all the Israelites accepted the good news. For

> ONCE WE KNOW THE PROMISES THAT HAVE BEEN PLACED IN THE WORD BY GOD HIMSELF, THEN WE HAVE THE BASIS FOR SEEING THEM BECOME REALITIES IN OUR LIVES.

Isaiah says, "Lord, who has believed our message?" Consequently, faith comes from hearing the message, and the message is heard through the word of Christ. (Romans 10:13–17 NIV)

If we had never read or been told that salvation is not just about making heaven our home but also about getting some heaven to us here on earth—remember, we are to pray, *"Your kingdom come, your will be done on earth, as it is in heaven"* (Matthew 6:10 NIV)—we would never know to expect that, either. If we don't know what's on the menu, so to speak, we won't even realize what's available! Once we know the promises that have been placed in the Word by God Himself, then we have the basis for seeing them become realities in our lives. The Word tells us repeatedly that, in addition to being our Savior for all eternity, the Lord wants to bring us divine deliverance, healing, peace, joy, and prosperity in this lifetime—*"life…to the full"* (John 10:10 NIV)!

Get Your Daily Dose of God's Mercy, Grace, Favor, Equipping, and Anointing

Every day, I make a point to pray the mercy, grace, favor, equipping, and anointing of God into my life. We hear those terms so often that we tend to discount their meanings, so let's look at a few Scriptures that talk about these blessings in order to gain a better appreciation of their significance.

> *Let us then approach the throne of grace with confidence, so that we may receive **mercy** and find grace to help us in our time of need.* (Hebrews 4:16 NIV, emphasis added)

> *For surely, O LORD, you bless the righteous; you surround them with your **favor** as with a shield.* (Psalm 5:12 NIV, emphasis added)

> *All Scripture is God-breathed and is useful for teaching, rebuking, correcting and training in righteousness, so that the man of God may be thoroughly **equipped** for every good work.* (2 Timothy 3:16–17 NIV, emphasis added)

*You have an **anointing** from the Holy One, and all of you know the truth.*   (1 John 2:20 NIV, emphasis added)

Let's take a look at what these terms mean as defined by *Merriam-Webster's 11th Collegiate Dictionary.*

Mercy: "compassion or forbearance shown especially to an offender or to one subject to one's power;…a blessing that is an act of divine favor or compassion."

We don't have to be perfect; we just have to be on the right path.

Grace: "unmerited divine assistance given humans for their regeneration or sanctification." Grace is an unmerited, unearned favor from God. We don't deserve it. We haven't earned it. It's not because of our stellar performance; it's because of His immense love for us!

Grace is the ability of God coming upon us and enabling us to do what we cannot do for ourselves.

Favor: "friendly regard shown toward another especially by a superior: approving consideration or attention." God's favor surrounds us like a shield, attracting all of the blessings that He desires for us. It causes people and events to move on our behalf, beyond what is natural or expected.

Equipping: *to equip* means "to furnish for service or action by appropriate provisioning; dress, array; to make ready: prepare." Where God guides, He provides. What He calls us to do, He equips us to do. The equipping of the Lord encompasses both the external and internal aspects of our lives.

Anointing: *to anoint* means "to smear or rub with oil or an oily substance; to apply oil to as a sacred rite especially for consecration." This is the process by which God applies His super to our natural. The anointing transports us out of the confines and limitations of the natural realm and into the unlimited, unending realm of the supernatural. The anointing connects our needs to God's solutions, our weaknesses to His strength, and our limited abilities and resources to His never-ending equipping and supply!

It is essential for us to comprehend what God has promised in order to enter into the fullness of it. Our God will never leave us out there all alone on a ledge. He fully intends to fill us completely with His mercy and grace, shower us with His unprecedented favor, and endue us with His anointing, abilities, and equipping. All we have to do is to ask Him, believe Him, and then enter in!

The Names of God

What's in a name? The names of God reveal the nature of God and express who He is and who He wants to be in our lives. His names show us what He wants to do for us, as well as what He has already done for us. One way to discover some of God's promises of provision to us is by becoming familiar with His names, which He uses to reveal aspects of Himself.

We will cover these titles in greater detail in a later chapter, but here is a brief list of some of God's names and their significance. God promises that He will be:

- Jehovah Tsidkenu: The God who is our righteousness.
- Jehovah M'Kaddesh: The God who sanctifies us.
- Jehovah Shalom: The God who fills us with His peace.
- Jehovah Shammah: The God who is there for whatever we need, whenever we need it.
- Jehovah Rophe: The God who heals us.
- Jehovah Nissi: The God who is our victory and protection.
- Jehovah Rohi: The God who is our shepherd and guide.
- Jehovah Jireh: The God who provides for all our needs.

Often, when people come to me to pray about a major issue in their lives, whether financial, physical, spiritual, or other, they ask the Lord to give them more faith to believe for a miracle. I always point them to the Source of their faith and the Source of their miracle—God Himself! In knowing Him, His Word, His promises, and His nature, we automatically begin to understand His immense love for each of us, which is the foundation of all faith and miracles. So, rather than just seeking a miracle, first seek the Miracle Worker!

Again, when Jesus taught His disciples to pray, He instructed them to begin by addressing the Lord as *"our Father."* (See, for example, Matthew

6:9.) While God is majestic and most high, He is also a loving, kind, attentive Father to you and me. He holds the entire universe together; He knows each and every thing that takes place at each and every moment; and yet He is keenly aware of each and every thing about each of us. Even more wondrous is that He knows us and *still* wants to be intimately involved in every part of our lives! This is yet another one of God's wonderful promises to us!

When this truth becomes instilled in your heart, you realize that you don't have to come pleading and begging; rather, you come to God and simply enter into what He's already done for you. As we discuss several different names of God, let the Lord open your heart to a greater understanding of who He is. Let your heart touch His, and let His heart touch yours. Let the Spirit of God take you to a new dimension in your own spirit. Take the limits off your perception of God, and take the limits off of yourself.

Prayer and Promise Principles

- In order to take ownership of the truth, we first have to know what the truth—the Word of God—promises to us. We can't lay claim to what we don't even know exists!

- God's names reveal aspects of His nature, and one way to discover God's promises of provision to us is by becoming familiar with His names.

- The names of God assure us that He is the God who is our righteousness; the God who sanctifies us; the God who fills us with His peace, the God who is there for whatever we need, whenever we need it; the God who heals us; the God who provides for all our needs; the God who is our victory and protection; and the God who is our shepherd and guide.

- God knows all about us and *still* wants to be intimately involved in every part of our lives!

Chapter Ten

Step Three: Personalize the Promises

In order to believe for God's promises to manifest in our lives, it is important that we personalize them and make them relevant to our particular situations. One thing that all believers have in common, regardless of their unique circumstances, is that they all have dominion and authority because of their heavenly Father. (See Genesis 1:26–28; Luke 9:1–2.) The more that we understand and internalize this fact by taking ownership of it, the greater dominion we will walk in, and the more we will feel entitled to possess God's promises.

Types of Learning and the Study of the Word

I want to digress for a moment to give you some insight about the process of taking ownership of the promises of God in His Word. In education, business, and other realms, there are many different styles of teaching. Certain teaching methods have been proven to multiply the effectiveness of the instruction and to increase the learners' absorption and retention of the material.

You might think that the student's comprehension depends on the way the teacher communicates or teaches the subject matter, and that's true—to a degree. But just as important is the way the student hears, receives, and digests the material. There are several primary distinctions among learners and what teaching methods are most effective for them. These are passive learners, active learners, and engaged learners.

Passive Learners

Passive learners listen but are easily distracted; they tend to pay minimal attention to the lesson and are unlikely to take notes. They listen as if the teaching is factual but not relevant to their personal lives. They're hearing but not absorbing; they're learning but not connecting what they learn to their own lives. It has been proven that passive learners will absorb and retain about 30 percent of what they have been taught.

Active Learners

Active learners listen attentively, take notes, and make a genuine attempt to retain the information they are taught. They are more diligent and intentional about learning than passive learners, but they still fail to connect the material they learn to their own lives. Active learners typically absorb and retain about 50 percent of what they have been taught.

Engaged Learners

Engaged learners listen attentively, take notes, and also participate in the lesson by posing questions and discussing the material. The verbal component to their learning seems to seal the information more permanently in their minds. Taking in the information and applying it to their own lives seals it even more deeply in their memories, for the mind retains what it finds to be relevant and not random. These learners take ownership of the truths they learn by making them personal, and it has been proven that engaged learners will absorb and retain about 90 percent of what they have been taught!

Be an Engaged Learner of the Word

The Bible says that the truth we *know* will set us free. As we go deeper in the Word, the Word goes deeper into us. It starts to determine our response to every situation; it comes to mind almost as naturally as breathing.

When we verbally engage in the Word or respond to a teaching, it drives that truth deep down inside of us so that we'll never forget it. How many times do we hear something and then forget it immediately afterward? How many newspaper or magazine articles do we read through once and never think about again? How much information do we hear that just goes in one ear and out the other, with no effect whatsoever on our lives?

The Word of God is not just another meaningless, irrelevant storybook. It is a supernatural book handwritten by God Himself through His prophets and inspired writers. It is filled with life-changing, problem-solving, devil-blasting, burden-removing, yoke-destroying, poverty-breaking, prosperity-releasing, debt-canceling abundance, overflow, outpouring, and anointing that can break every curse and release every blessing!

God's Promises Apply to You, Personally

When you read Scripture, every time you see a "thee," "thy," "you," or other second-person pronoun that isn't referring to God, try inserting your own name to make it personal, to allow the truth to sink into your soul. Take what Jesus spoke to His disciples in Luke 12:7, for example. This verse reads, *"Indeed, the very hairs of your head are all numbered. Don't be afraid; you are worth more than many sparrows"* (NIV). To personalize this verse, I would read it like this: "Indeed, the very hairs of my head are numbered. Don't be afraid; I am worth more than many sparrows." I could also say, "Indeed, the very hairs of Tiz's head are numbered. Don't be afraid; Tiz is worth more than many sparrows."

As you read Scriptures about God's covenant of blessing, insert your own name to personalize His promises. The assurances of Scripture are for the entire world—and that includes you and me! Also, don't be shy about bold verbal expression. Say "amen" out loud! *Amen* actually means, "So be it in my life." Boldly declare, "Yes! I believe and receive that word!" By involving yourself verbally and emotionally—by taking ownership of the truth—you're going to leap from 30 percent to 90 percent absorption and retention of what you read in the Scriptures. You'll be an engaged learner of the Word. Can you shout amen? Wow, I can hear the shackles falling off your mind and hitting the ground *right now!*

Practice with Scriptures That Assure You of Your Dominion and Authority

As we go through this next section and examine Scriptures on the authority of the believer, let the reality of what God is saying really sink into your heart, mind, and soul. Even if you've heard these Scriptures countless times before, read them as if God Himself is talking to you personally, because that's exactly what He's doing!

That's how we begin to take personal ownership of the authority that the Lord wants us to walk in. Let's get the ball rolling right now! Read the following Scriptures out loud and insert your own name within them.

- *"Thou madest (<u>your name</u>) to have dominion over the works of thy hands; thou hast put all things under (<u>your name</u>'s) feet"* (Psalm 8:6).

- *"Verily I say unto (<u>your name</u>), whatsoever (<u>your name</u>) shall bind on earth shall be bound in heaven: and whatsoever (<u>your name</u>) shall loose on earth shall be loosed in heaven"* (Matthew 18:18).

- *"Truly, truly, I say to (<u>your name</u>), he who believes in Me, the works that I do shall (<u>your name</u>) do also; and greater works than these shall (<u>your name</u>) do; because I go to the Father. And whatever (<u>your name</u>) ask[s] in My name, that will I do, that the Father may be glorified in the Son. If (<u>your name</u>) ask[s] Me anything in My name, I will do it"* (John 14:12–14 NASB).

- *"I have given (<u>your name</u>) authority over all the power of the Enemy"* (Luke 10:19 TLB).

- *"When Jesus had called the Twelve together, he gave them power and authority to drive out all demons and to cure diseases, and he sent them out to preach the kingdom of God and to heal the sick"* (Luke 9:1–2 NIV). This includes you and me, too!

These are just a few examples of how to make the Word of God and its promises relevant and powerful in your life. Matthew 7:7 assures us, *"Ask, and it shall be given you; seek, and ye shall find; knock, and it shall be opened unto you."* Verses 9–11 go on to ask,

What man is there of you, whom if his son ask bread, will he give him a stone? Or if he ask him a fish, will he give him a serpent? If ye then, being evil, know how to give good gifts unto your children, how much more shall your Father which is in heaven give good gifts to them that ask him?

God Wills That We Walk in Total Power and Authority

It is quite evident from the above sampling of Scriptures that the Lord has entrusted us with complete and total power and authority over the works of the enemy. It is God's intent for His children—you and me—to conquer and take dominion over every force of darkness and every attack of the enemy in every area of our lives!

IT IS GOD'S INTENT FOR HIS CHILDREN—YOU AND ME—TO CONQUER AND TAKE DOMINION OVER EVERY FORCE OF DARKNESS AND EVERY ATTACK OF THE ENEMY IN EVERY AREA OF OUR LIVES!

"Whatsoever ye shall bind on earth shall be bound in heaven: and whatsoever ye shall loose on earth shall be loosed in heaven" (Matthew 18:18) is quite an extraordinary statement! It is not a vague hope; it's an absolute promise! Are we meant to take it as a literal promise from God's mouth? I am completely convinced that we are! However, most of us would have to admit that the circumstances of our lives are not exactly confirming this promise. But don't let that discourage you! Remember, our faith walk is a journey. God is changing us *"from glory to glory"* (2 Corinthians 3:18). We may not be all the way there yet, but we are definitely on the right path!

Let me explain to you a little more about binding and loosing. The word *loose* comes from the Greek word *luo* (*Strong's* #3089). *Luo* can be defined as to dissolve, to break up, to destroy, to melt, to put off, to release, to free from bondage, to discharge from prison, to restore to health, to liberate, to undo the chains, and to set free. Spiritually speaking, it means to destroy completely the power of the enemy.

The word *bind* is derived from the Greek word *deo* (*Strong's* #1210), which means to chain down, to hinder, to tie up hand and foot, to keep in bonds, to imprison, to take captive, or to fetter a furious person. In classic Greek, it was used as a term for putting a leash on a dog or a wild animal.

These two terms paint a vivid picture. The Lord has entrusted us with an incredible privilege and responsibility. He has given us complete power and authority to bind and loosen all the strategies, assaults, and power of Satan. We don't need to let the enemy have one ounce of dominion in our hearts, our minds, our physical bodies, our families, or our world. We have been given extraordinary supernatural authority to stand in the gap and see the enemy's strongholds torn down. This authority does not come from who we are but from who we are *through* our God. It comes from our knowing, understanding, and executing God's Word and dominion, through the name and the blood of our Savior, Jesus Christ.

We are given authority over *all* the works of the enemy through:

- The blood of Jesus Christ. (See Revelation 12:11.)
- The name of Jesus. (See Mark 16:17.)
- The Word of God. (See Ephesians 6:17.)
- The confession of our mouths. (See Revelation 12:11.)

In Larry's book *Free at Last*, he includes a section called "Seven Places Jesus Shed His Blood" in which he tells how Jesus shed His blood not just once, but seven times. Each time, He won something back for us: our willpower, our health, our prosperity, our dominion over the things we touch, our dominion over the places we walk, our joy, and our deliverance from inner hurts and iniquities.[4] To put this teaching succinctly, the blood shed by Jesus, our Savior, redeemed us from the dominion of Satan and from every one of his strategies, weapons, and attacks.

Specific Promises for Specific Problems

It is vital to apply God's promises specifically to our individual lives when we pray in our "prayer closets." The Bible tells us, *"When thou prayest, enter into thy closet, and when thou hast shut thy door, pray to the Father*

---

[4] See Huch, *Free at Last*, 108–173.

which is in secret; and thy Father which seeth in secret shall reward thee openly" (Matthew 6:6).

Our prayer closets can be likened to the pharmacy dispensary in a hospital. You, the nurse or doctor, are permitted access to the hospital dispensary, where you can submit requests for the specific medicines and supplies you need, obtain them, and then walk out with them. If you come into the dispensary with a need for penicillin, you obtain penicillin. If you come in with a need for bandages, you procure bandages. That is the picture of how we are to see our prayer closets. We have been given the freedom to walk into the throne room of God (His dispensary), submit our requests, and then obtain and walk out with the provisions for our needs and the solutions to our problems. Thank God that our prayers will never fall upon deaf ears! And, we will never walk away from God's throne room empty-handed! He promises that if we will come into our prayer closets and spend time with Him, trusting in His ability to help us, He will answer those prayers and reward us openly.

> WE WILL NEVER WALK AWAY FROM GOD'S THRONE ROOM EMPTY-HANDED!

Our salvation encompasses so much more than eternal life. Again, my husband says it like this: "Salvation is not just about getting us into heaven for all of eternity, but it's also about getting some heaven into us while we're still here on earth!" One of the Greek words translated "salvation" in the New Testament is *diasozo* (*Strong's* #1295), which means to make thoroughly sound or whole.

In the Bible, simply touching Jesus brought healing and salvation to many people. *"People brought all their sick to [Jesus] and begged him to let the sick just touch the edge of his cloak, and all who touched him were healed ["made perfectly whole" KJV]"* (Matthew 14:35–36 NIV). *"Made perfectly whole"* is the translation of *diasozo*. In other words, after touching Jesus, the formerly sick had nothing missing and nothing broken.

As we discussed in the previous chapter, the Lord has revealed His nature and His will for us through His names. Our God takes care of His children in every way—He always has, and He always will. He not only desires to give us eternal life, but He also desires to be our Healer, our Provider, our Victory, our Peace, our Shepherd, and our Guide. His name Jehovah Shammah tells us that He is whatever we need Him to be, whenever we need Him to be it! Whatever this life throws at us, our God already has it covered! Whatever issues we face in this world, our God has an answer for us in His Word!

What is it that you need? Do you need healing of your body, your emotions, or your mind? Maybe you need help in your marriage or with raising your children. Maybe you need a financial miracle. You may walk into your prayer closet with all kinds of needs, but you're going to walk out with all kinds of answers!

Again, sometimes, we have to knock, keep on knocking, and then knock some more! And then—guess what? If we still haven't received a complete answer, we knock, keep on knocking, and then knock some more! Repeat as many times as is necessary. I wish, as I know you do, too, that every time we prayed, we would see instantaneous, miraculous results! In a perfect world, our lives would play out like half-hour sitcoms on TV—every problem would be compactly presented and neatly solved within a thirty-minute time slot! But in the real world, for various reasons, it usually takes a little longer and requires a little more effort than it does on television.

Again, while you will sometimes see the answer immediately, there will be times when you have to wait a while before God gives you an answer. Don't allow a delayed response to worry you, for we are assured that God *"acts on behalf of those who wait for him"* (Isaiah 64:4 NIV).

David had to remind himself to wait patiently for God. In Psalm 27:14, he wrote, *"Wait on the LORD: be of good courage, and he shall strengthen thine heart: wait, I say, on the LORD."* And in Psalm 37:7, he said, *"Rest in the Lord, and wait patiently for him."*

The prophet Micah was confident that the Lord would reply, even as he waited: *"I watch in hope for the LORD, I wait for God my Savior; my God will hear me"* (Micah 7:7 NIV).

Know this: the moment that you pray, God hears you and begins to move on your behalf. Whether our miraculous answers come instantaneously or whether they take a bit longer to manifest, we can stand firmly on God's Word and His promises. Hebrews 10:23 exhorts us to *"hold fast the profession of our faith without wavering; (for he is faithful that promised)."* When you ask God to do something, He will never, ever turn a deaf ear to you. He will never, ever ignore you.

At times, we give birth to a miracle immediately. Other times, the miracle is conceived, and we are pregnant with the promises that will be birthed at a later time. Either way, you can be sure that God will prove faithful. He has *you* on His mind right now, and His promises of blessing are for you!

PRAYER AND PROMISE PRINCIPLES

- To believe for God's promises to manifest in our lives, it is important that we personalize them and make them relevant to our particular situations.

- When we verbally engage in the Word or respond to a teaching, it drives that truth deep down inside of us so that we'll never forget it. We must be engaged learners of God's Word!

- The Lord has entrusted us with complete and total power and authority over the works of the enemy.

- God promises that if we will come into our prayer closets and spend time with Him, trusting in His ability to help us, He will answer those prayers and reward us openly.

- Whatever this life throws at us, our God already has it covered! Whatever issues we face in this world, our God has an answer for us in His Word!

Chapter Eleven

STEP FOUR: ALIGN YOUR THOUGHTS, WORDS, AND ACTIONS WITH GOD'S WORD

Paul wrote in 2 Corinthians 10:3–5,

> *For though we walk in the flesh, we do not war after the flesh: (for the weapons of our warfare are not carnal, but mighty through God to the pulling down of strong holds;) casting down imaginations, and every high thing that exalteth itself against the knowledge of God, and bringing into captivity every thought to the obedience of Christ.*

The first point he was making is that our battle is in the spiritual realm and therefore must be fought with spiritual weapons. His second point was that our most important weapons are what we think, say, and do. We have to align our thoughts, words, and actions with the Word of God!

No power of hell can stand against the power of the Word of God. However, we become susceptible to the devil's schemes when we allow negative thoughts, words, and actions to prevail in our lives, for these weaken our defenses.

On the contrary, positive, faith-filled thoughts, words, and actions lift us up and strengthen us against the power of the enemy. I'm not advocating a complete denial of adversity—we've got to be aware and in the moment— but we can think, speak, and act in constructive ways that keep us from succumbing to the devil's attacks.

Aligning Your Thoughts with God's Word

Let's begin by talking about lining up our thoughts with God's thoughts, as expressed in His Word. Every effective prayer or assault against the enemy is going to originate from within us. The power is birthed from our knowing God and being familiar with His Word. When we know Him, we trust Him and have faith in Him. When we know His Word, it becomes alive within us, releasing faith that moves mountains! (See, for example, Matthew 17:20.) This confidence and faith produce prayers that touch the *heart* of God and move the *hand* of God!

> INSTEAD OF OUR TREMBLING IN FEAR AT THE POWER OF THE ENEMY, THE ENEMY WILL BE TREMBLING IN FEAR AT THE POWER OF GOD'S CHILDREN—YOU AND ME!

The more that we comprehend this, the more we will be able to drive back Satan's forces and release all of God's blessings. By the renewing of our minds by the Word (see Romans 12:2), we are transformed more and more into the image and likeness of our God. The ongoing result is this: instead of our trembling in fear at the power of the enemy, the enemy will be trembling in fear at the power of God's children— you and me! I am not trying to just create a cute little cliché that we can casually quote. Rather, I am trying to create a literal picture of the impact that we can have within the spiritual dimension.

Change Your Thinking, Change Your Life

Our authority comes naturally as we saturate our minds and thoughts with the promises of God. Proverbs 4:23 tells us, *"Keep ["guard" NIV] your heart with all diligence, for out of it spring the issues of life"* (NKJV). In other words, out of our thinking and our spirits comes every outcome of our futures and our lives. Change your thinking and you'll change your life! Another one of my favorite sayings is, "It is impossible to take a journey on the inside and stand still on the outside." Be assured that as we build up our spirits with the promises of God, these promises will soon begin to manifest as realities in our lives!

Believe the Right Report

Let's return for a moment to the Scripture that says, *"Many are called, but few are chosen"* (Matthew 22:14). Times of hardship and challenge are pivotal points in our faith journeys, and those of us who decide to be *"chosen"*—the sons and daughters of God—must choose to believe the reports of our God rather than the reports of the enemy. I love the song by Martha Munizzi that shouts, "Whose report will you believe?" I choose—and I know you do, too—to believe that *"greater is he that is within [me], than he that is in the world"* (1 John 4:4). Say it with attitude: "Greater is He who is within me than he who is *chasing* me!" Every time that we choose to believe and trust in God's Word rather than our circumstances, we move to a higher level of faith.

Control Your Thoughts and Win the Battle in Your Mind

Our minds are the battlegrounds for spiritual warfare, and the battle is won or lost in our minds before it is won or lost in the physical world. I cannot emphasize strongly enough how important it is for us to control our thoughts! As the apostle Paul put it, we must *"take captive every thought to make it obedient to Christ"* (2 Corinthians 10:5 NIV).

> WHEN DOUBT AND FEAR THREATEN TO CONSUME YOUR MIND, PICTURE YOURSELF PULLING YOUR THOUGHTS INTO ALIGNMENT WITH THE WORD OF GOD. PULL DOWN THOSE THOUGHTS THAT CONTRADICT GOD'S WILL AND HIS PROMISES.

When doubt and fear threaten to consume your mind, picture yourself actually pulling your thoughts into alignment with the Word of God. Pull down those thoughts that contradict God's will and His promises. Determine to resist and reject any thoughts that don't match God's promises. Then, picture yourself replacing those negative doubts with faith, confidence, and knowledge of His Word.

It is crucial to cast down doubt and fear and align our thoughts with the Word. We have already discussed this passage, but let's review it again, for it is particularly important in our prayers for financial prosperity. Second Corinthians 10:3–5 says,

> *For though we live in the world, we do not wage war as the world does. The weapons we fight with are not the weapons of the world. On the contrary, they have divine power to demolish strongholds. We demolish arguments and every pretension that sets itself up against the knowledge of God, and we take captive every thought to make it obedient to Christ.* (NIV)

When faced with financial hardship, for example, saturate your mind and consume your thoughts with what God has to say about your financial picture. We have this assurance from Paul in Philippians 4:19: *"My God shall supply all your need according to his riches in glory by Christ Jesus."* Our God is surrounded in heaven by vast riches, resources, and wealth, and He assures us that we can count on Him to share His supply with us. He will wire funds to us from His account to ours to meet our daily needs! So, settle your mind, your thoughts, and your emotions. Create an arena of faith, hope, confidence, and expectancy.

Aligning Your Words with God's Word

You've probably heard the saying, "Confession brings possession." I absolutely believe that it's true. Many people mock "name-it-and-claim-it" believers, and I concede that some people take this notion to an unbiblical extreme. Many of us have seen, if not participated in, fervent displays of "faith" that seem to go overboard. I'm not talking about when the world calls you ridiculous because of your declarations of faith, nor am I talking about living in denial of the reality of life. But I am talking about lining up our thoughts, our confessions, and our lifestyles in accordance with the promises of God.

Years ago, a local pastor ridiculed Larry and me because of our teachings on faith. He mockingly called us the "name-it-and-claim-it" pastors of the "blab-it-and-grab-it" church. He later confessed to us that his wife had confronted him about this and said, "What is the alternative—to preach doom and gloom? To discourage people from believing God so that they face life the same way as unbelievers? As pastors, shouldn't we be giving people the hope that God will fulfill His promises to His children?" The pastor told us that this was a rude awakening to the fact that he had become cynical and negative about the faith message. From that point on, he began to teach and live in a new dimension of faith.

I can't guarantee you that every time you speak out by faith and lay claim to something, it will come true immediately. Our God is not a genie in a bottle who obeys our every command and makes all our wishes come true. I *can* guarantee you, though, that without determined faith, you will never see many of God's promises come true.

The Bible tells us that *"without faith it is impossible to please* [God]" (Hebrews 11:6). I would much rather be accused of trusting God too much than of not trusting Him enough! My motto is this: We can never out-trust our God. The more faith-demands we put upon His promises, the more He will manifest His Word in our lives!

> I CAN'T GUARANTEE YOU THAT EVERY TIME YOU SPEAK OUT BY FAITH AND LAY CLAIM TO SOMETHING, IT WILL COME TRUE IMMEDIATELY. I CAN GUARANTEE YOU, THOUGH, THAT WITHOUT DETERMINED FAITH, YOU WILL NEVER SEE MANY OF GOD'S PROMISES COME TRUE.

So, how about making a bold confession together right now? Say this out loud with me: "I absolutely believe that my God is watching over His Word and His promises in every area of my life! I know that His Word *will not* and *cannot* return to Him void—without accomplishing what it was sent to do! I am standing confidently upon my Father's promise to me that He will make good on every one of His promises for my life. Amen and amen!"

Making confessions such as this one is one way that we take ownership of the promises of God, making them our personal possessions. This is how we enter into the realm where it's no longer us chasing down the blessings of God but the blessings of God chasing us down!

Claim God's Promises

Larry and I have learned that the way we discuss an issue is extremely critical in determining the outcome. When we're talking about something, we focus on viewing it through the eyes of the Lord in order to discover His answers and solutions. Even if the issue is particularly negative or controversial, we always discuss it in light of God's help, and we always conclude the conversation by claiming God's promises.

Worry comes from viewing our situations without God in the picture. But faith is worry that has said its prayers! Hope is doubt that has said its prayers! And optimism is pessimism that chose to believe God!

AGREEING WITH GOD IN PRAYER—TRULY BELIEVING THAT GOD WILL FULFILL HIS PROMISES AND GRANT WHAT WE ASK—IS JUST AS IMPORTANT AND EFFECTIVE AS HAVING ANOTHER PERSON WITH WHOM TO AGREE IN PRAYER.

Our words must line up in unity in order to move us into the blessings of God. You've probably heard about the power of agreement in prayer. This concept comes from Matthew 18:19–20, where Jesus said,

If two of you shall agree on earth as touching any thing that they shall ask, it shall be done for them of my Father which is in heaven. For where two or three are gathered together in my name, there am I in the midst of them.

Thank God for the times when we have someone to agree with us in prayer and intercession. Larry and I do this all the time, and we see many amazing breakthroughs. However, I believe that there is another level of meaning to this Scripture. Agreeing with God in prayer—truly believing that God will fulfill His promises and grant what we ask—is just as important and effective as having another person with whom to agree in prayer. We need to align our entire selves with the promises in God's Word. Our thoughts, words, and actions must line up in unity in order to move us into the blessings of God. Therefore, we need to develop a habit of being positive in what we say.

Speak Positive Words

We have to control our tongues. Make a determined effort to avoid speaking negative words and complaints. Speak only positive, faith-filled words—not just any positive words, but *the* positive Word of God! God's Word holds the power to create good things and to change our circumstances. Proverbs 18:21 says that *"the tongue has the power of life and death, and those who love it will eat its fruit"* (NIV). The Lord has entrusted us with an incredibly powerful gift—the power of life and death within our own words!

Keep in mind that every word you speak has creative power to produce something, either positive or negative! Larry and I frequently say, "If you're saying it, you're praying it!" Yes, this truth is somewhat sobering, but it can and should also be exciting and empowering. You and I don't have to live within the financial boundaries and physical limitations of

> **IF YOU'RE SAYING IT, YOU'RE PRAYING IT!**

this world. Through our prayers and through confessing and claiming the promises in God's Word, we can tap into God's supernatural provision, help, and blessings. So, make up your mind right now to put a guard on your mouth. No more negative words or complaints. Only the promises of God should come out of those lips!

Prophesy the Word of God

For more than thirty years, Larry and I have been practicing these principles of faith. We live in the same world that you do. We face many of the same challenges as everyone else.

But because we are continually pressing toward new levels in our lives, ministry, and business, we are continually placing higher demands on the promises of God. As we are challenged to expand our ministry to touch more people with the gospel, we are also challenged to believe God for the increase in finances to enable us to do this. We have had to learn to trust Him more and more every year, and we have also experienced His miraculous provision more and more every year. The more you decide to trust Him for, the more ways He will prove Himself faithful to you!

Larry and I don't just preach this from the pulpit. We live it behind the scenes, too. We don't just speak positive words when the microphone is on. We have trained ourselves to speak the positive Word all day, every day. And it works! If we don't see a solution, we create one by speaking God's promises. The best way to predict your future is to prophecy your future through the Word of God. This faith stuff really works!

Aligning Your Actions with God's Word

We have to physically act in agreement with the promises of God. If we say that we're believing God for a miracle, then we need to act accordingly. If we're believing and confessing for a miracle, then let's carry ourselves with the confidence that we already have that miracle.

Pray

The most obvious action we can take to align our lives with God's Word is to pray. It does us no good to study the Bible and learn about prayer if we don't actually pray! This is a little story that I get a kick out of. A church advisory committee was voting on some very important church issues, such as what color the new carpet should be and what size the new windows should be. As all of the men and women were arguing back and forth, one dear little saint spoke up and suggested, "Why don't we quit arguing among ourselves and pray and ask God what to do?" After a long silence, the main church elder proclaimed, "Oh, dear God, has it come to this?"

Let's not make prayer our last resort. Let's make it our first response! Too often, people use prayer like a 9-1-1 emergency call. They don't pray until they find themselves in a crisis situation. Then, they make a 9-1-1 call to heaven and hope for a quick rescue.

I once saw a church sign with the message, "Ask God to rescue you." Well, that's great—thank God, He will rescue us—but I want us to get into the habit of "preventative" prayer. It isn't too different from preventative health—deliberate, healthy choices that prevent or decrease the likelihood of medical problems as opposed to living and eating recklessly in ways that will cause them and have us searching for cures. The same principle underlies the idea of preventative prayer. Rather than waiting until a crisis emerges and then praying for a cure or a miracle from heaven, how about praying daily to activate God's promises and prevent crises from occurring in the first place?

For example, as parents, let's not leave our children open to the temptations and attacks of the enemy. Let's not wait until they're on dangerous ground to intercede for them. Instead, let's pray for them and cover their minds, spirits, and bodies so that the world can never gain even a single foothold in their lives! Let's not wait until we're sick and need a miracle to learn about divine healing. Rather, let's cover ourselves and our loved ones with divine health and long life every day, preventing sickness from even thinking about attacking us! Let's not wait until we're in the midst of a financial crisis, needing God to rescue us; let's call upon Jehovah Jireh, our Provider, every morning to meet the needs that we will experience that day. Let's not sit idle and watch our marriages disintegrate and be torn apart; let's be proactive in prayer! Pray over your spouse and your marriage, bind the attacks of the enemy of your soul, and release the peace, joy, harmony, and blessings that God has for you. Many times, prayer will block an attack of the enemy before you even know it's coming!

> RATHER THAN WAITING UNTIL A CRISIS EMERGES AND THEN PRAYING FOR A CURE OR A MIRACLE FROM HEAVEN, HOW ABOUT PRAYING DAILY TO ACTIVATE GOD'S PROMISES AND PREVENT CRISES FROM OCCURRING IN THE FIRST PLACE?

Carry Yourself with Confidence That Miracles Are Coming

Our body language can communicate even more clearly than our verbal expressions how we are feeling or what we believe. By reading an individual's body language—how he carries himself, how he appears on the outside—you can often tell what's happening on the inside. We speak volumes when we are standing erect versus slouching, looking attentive versus looking bored, engaging in conversation or clamming up with apathy, boldly going forth or timidly hanging back, smiling or frowning, and so forth. There is an obvious difference between the countenance of an individual when he has succeeded at something as opposed to when he has failed. Are you getting the picture? Let's work on lining up our body language with our thoughts and words of success and victory. Let's present a united front that shows we are pressing through to our miracles. Let's use our bodies to prove our belief that our God is working on our behalf!

I heard a story about one of the evangelists from the early 1900s who was facing a multitude of endless battles and had grown quite weary. He allowed himself to fall into a deep depression. For several weeks, he wouldn't leave the house or talk to anyone. Finally, one morning, his wife decided that she had to do something to break his downward cycle. So, she came downstairs dressed all in black with a veil covering her face, as if in mourning. Her husband saw her and exclaimed, "Who died?" She replied, "Apparently, from the way you've been acting, God did!"

It's often said that actions speak louder than words. Let's make sure that negative actions don't drown out the voice of the Lord and the positive promises from His Word.

Face Each Day with the Attitude, Countenance, and Posture of a Winner

Let's agree right now to face each day and the future with the attitudes, countenances, and postures of winners! No more moping, moaning, groaning, pouting, pity-seeking, wining, grouchy, sad-sack, slouched-shoulders, droopy, dragging-your-feet, sniffling, downcast, mournful behavior! Let's see…did I miss anything?

How do you think I know about all of these negative, destructive, unproductive types of behaviors? Because I have personally faced, dealt with, and conquered (or am attempting to conquer) all of them!

Let's make a conscious effort to carry ourselves like we've just won the lottery. Hold your head up high. Stand tall, even if you're short. Put a smile on your face, a twinkle in your eye, and a spring in your step. Show some spunk in your attitude, because you're on the verge of a great and mighty breakthrough! You are positioned for an incredible future! You are about to experience blessings beyond your wildest dreams!

Ephesians 3:20 assures us that our God *"is able to do exceeding abundantly above all that we ask or think, according to the power that worketh in us."* We are packed with dynamite power to prosper and excel, to walk in divine favor every day, and to connect God's supernatural provision and blessings to our natural world!

> SHOW SOME SPUNK IN YOUR ATTITUDE, BECAUSE YOU'RE ON THE VERGE OF A GREAT AND MIGHTY BREAKTHROUGH! YOU ARE POSITIONED FOR AN INCREDIBLE FUTURE!

The Process of Alignment Is an Exciting Journey

We need to understand the powerful force of our thoughts, words, and actions. But we also need to remember that the spiritual walk is an exciting journey! We can give ourselves a "check-up from the neck up" without piling guilt and condemnation on ourselves, which will only land us in therapy to get through everything that we just dug up!

"We all, with open face beholding as in a glass the glory of the Lord, are changed into the same image from glory to glory, even as by the Spirit of the Lord" (2 Corinthians 3:18). If you make a mistake, make it right. If you fall flat on your face, get up, brush yourself off, and keep going. If you blow it, repent and plan to do better next time. If it happens again, repeat the preceding steps! Always remember: God is not pointing a finger of accusation at you. He's reaching out a hand to help you. Never stop growing, stretching, or reaching. We are on a wonderful journey that will never end!

In the next part of our journey, we will explore the Lord's Prayer, which provides us a model for the most dynamic prayers possible. Now that we know about God's promises to us and our entitlement to receive them, and now that we understand how to take ownership of those promises, let's learn to pray in a way that incorporates these lessons and will lead us into deeper, more intimate relationships with our Lord and Savior.

Remember, guard your heart. Guard your words. Guard your actions. Enjoy the journey. Expect miracles. Experience His wonder.

Prayer and Promise Principles

- We must choose to believe the reports of our God rather than the reports of the enemy.

- Our minds are the battlegrounds for spiritual warfare, and the battle is won or lost in our minds before it is won or lost in the physical world.

- God's Word holds the power to create good things and to change our circumstances.

- We can never out-trust our God. The more faith-demands we put upon His promises, the more He will manifest His Word in our lives!

- Many times, prayer will block an attack of the enemy before you even know it's coming!

- Always remember: God is not pointing a finger of accusation at you. He's reaching out a hand to help you.

THE LORD'S PRAYER

Chapter Twelve

THE LORD'S PRAYER

There is no better example of how to pray than the example set by Jesus. Let's look at the sixth chapter of Matthew. To set the stage, the disciples were with Jesus. They'd been watching Him pray. They'd been listening to Him pray. They'd been with Him when He had prayed for many people, and they'd witnessed the results of His prayers—miracle after miracle, from blind eyes seeing to lame legs walking to dead people coming back to life.

Having seen these things, the disciples said to Jesus, *"Lord, teach us to pray"* (Luke 11:1). These were men of prayer. They knew how to pray, but they didn't know how to pray with power. They didn't pray in a way that produced miraculous results. They wanted to go to a new level, and they knew that learning to pray as Jesus did would make them into men of powerful, life-changing prayer!

We are about to follow in the disciples' footsteps more than two thousand years later and attain a new level of seeing the manifestation of God's miraculous power. We're about to go into a new dimension of possessing the promises of God—not just once in a while, but on a continual basis!

"This, then, is how you should pray...."

The gospels of Matthew and Luke both include the account of Jesus teaching His disciples how to pray. He began this lesson by warning the disciples not to get caught up in all the pomp and circumstance of hypocritical, prideful, showy prayers. He said,

> When you pray, do not be like the hypocrites, for they love to pray standing in the synagogues and on the street corners to be seen by men. I tell you the truth, they have received their reward in full. But when you pray, go into your room, close the door and pray to your Father, who is unseen. Then your Father, who sees what is done in secret, will reward you. And when you pray, do not keep on babbling like pagans, for they think they will be heard because of their many words. Do not be like them, for your Father knows what you need before you ask him. (Matthew 6:5–8 NIV)

THE LORD'S PRAYER IS A SHORT AND SIMPLE OUTLINE THAT PRODUCES INCREDIBLE RESULTS BECAUSE IT ALIGNS WITH GOD'S WILL AND INSTRUCTIONS.

He went on to teach them how to pray from the heart in a way that touches the heart of God and obtains miraculous results. This instruction He began by saying, "This, then, is how you should pray" (Matthew 6:9 NIV).

It's wonderful to take the time and make the effort to go to church and to pray, but it's not about the quantity of prayers or the amount of time we spend praying—it's about the *quality* of prayer! Prayer is first and foremost about building a relationship with our Father. Everything else is secondary. Each part of the Lord's Prayer is not to be speedily recited by rote; rather, it is meant to accomplish a specific purpose within us and for us. The Lord's Prayer is a short and simple outline that produces incredible results because it aligns with God's will and instructions. It can be read or recited in a matter of seconds, but its brevity isn't the point. The point is to use the prayer as a guideline for meaningful times of heartfelt prayer and fellowship with our heavenly Father.

We're going to divide the prayer into smaller segments in order to study the meaning and intent of each. But first, let's briefly review the specific segments and introduce their import.

"Our Father which art in heaven, hallowed be thy name" (Matthew 6:9).

We start out, as Jesus did, by first honoring, worshipping, and praising the Lord simply for who He is. During this time of worship, we can do a number of things. We can thank Him for all that He has done, is doing, and will do for us. We can declare the names of God, praising Him for His unique attributes. Simply offer adoration to the King of Kings for His love, mercy, compassion…the list is unending!

"Thy kingdom come. Thy will be done in earth, as it is in heaven" (Matthew 6:10).

Next, we ask Jesus to work His perfect will in our lives, our families, our communities, our cities, our nations, and so forth. We appropriate all of the blessings that our Father intends for us to have, and we take authority over the works of the enemy, canceling every one of his plans for our futures.

We break the spirits of lack, poverty, and insufficiency over our finances, and we release all of God's supernatural provision of abundance and overflow! We break the spirit of containment over our checkbooks and call in every stored-up blessing that has been held back from our lives.

Together, we are going to break free from every bondage, addiction, sickness, or spirit of depression that the enemy or the world has tried to plague you with! We're going to break every stronghold that has held back the blessings of God with your name on them!

"Give us this day our daily bread" (Matthew 6:11).

After that, we present our requests to God, keeping in mind that He knows what we need long before we tell Him. We talk to Him about our needs, our pains, our hurts, our struggles, and we also pray for others.

"Forgive us our debts, as we forgive our debtors" (Matthew 6:12).

Following that, we repent of our sins and ask for God's forgiveness, which He freely gives. Notice that we claim to already have forgiven our *"debtors"*—those people who have sinned against us. If we fail to do this first before asking forgiveness of God, we won't receive it. Mark 11:25 says, *"When you stand praying, if you hold anything against anyone, forgive him, so that your Father in heaven may forgive you your sins"* (NIV). During this time of prayer, confess your sins to God and repent of them so that He may forgive you. Again, Matthew 6:14–15 tells us, *"For if you forgive men when they sin against you, your heavenly Father will also forgive you. But if you do not forgive men their sins, your Father will not forgive your sins"* (NIV).

"Lead us not into temptation, but deliver us from evil" (Matthew 6:13).

Next, we ask the Lord to strengthen our resistance against the enemy's attacks, namely, the temptation to fall into sin.

"For thine is the kingdom, and the power, and the glory, for ever. Amen" (Matthew 6:13).

I guarantee you that this kind of prayer will radically change your life forever. It's time to break free from the restraints, the burdens, and the bondages of the past! It's time to live in the dimension and dominion that the Lord has intended for His children! It's time for you to possess every one of the promises of God.

We Must Breathe In before We Can Breathe Out

As I said before, Larry and I are people of prayer. But after years of praying in the same way, our style of prayer took a huge turn. We had always viewed prayer as a time of intercession, and so we would spend the majority of our prayer time interceding for the needs of all of the people we pastored and also for the salvation of the world. We had a mind-set of focusing all our attention on the needs of others, and, as a result, we never really took the time to replenish our own spirits by praying for ourselves.

We came to a point in our lives where we were spiritually spent; the well had run dry, so to speak. Then, the Lord opened our eyes to a new way of praying. He showed us, through the Lord's Prayer, that before we can *give out*, we first have to *take in*. Biology teaches us the simple fact that before we can breathe out, we must first breathe in. Simply put, the time we invest in worshipping God feeds and replenishes our spirits, souls, and bodies. We "soak up" the Spirit of God, saturating ourselves with His strength, equipping, and anointing. He fills us up so that we can give to others!

As we praise Him for all that He is, faith automatically builds within us and naturally releases events in the miraculous realm. Therefore, it is extremely important for you to allow the Lord to saturate your mind and spirit with His mind and Spirit. We all live busy, hectic lives. Whether we're stay-at-home moms, students, businesspeople, ministers, or anything else, we are all constantly giving of ourselves. We need to take time out from our busy schedules to spend time with God, ceasing from pouring our energies into others and allowing God to pour replenishment and restoration back into us. Most of us are running on empty. We live our lives at warp speed, being pulled in a dozen different directions and running at an ever-increasing pace.

> THE TIME WE INVEST IN WORSHIPPING GOD FEEDS AND REPLENISHES OUR SPIRITS, SOULS, AND BODIES. WE "SOAK UP" THE SPIRIT OF GOD, SATURATING OURSELVES WITH HIS STRENGTH, EQUIPPING, AND ANOINTING.

The last thing we need is another task on our to-do list—including the task of prayer! Trust me; I'm extremely familiar with the feeling! I'm not trying to lay a burden or another task on any of us. My goal is to lighten our loads—through prayer! Prayer recharges our spiritual batteries, making us feel excited, energetic, enthusiastic, and full of life. Prayer fills us with anticipation for the day, not dread and weariness, because it enables us to tap into God's supernatural help, equipping, and resources. Just as our cars need to be refueled with gasoline in order to function, we have to stop and refuel with the Word of God and His supernatural empowering through prayer on a regular basis.

As soon as we wake up in the morning, all kinds of things and people begin calling out for our attention. Our families, our jobs, our ministries, our bills, our concerns, and our worries—all these are important things that legitimately demand and deserve our attention. But before we start focusing on other people or on all of the items on our to-do lists, let's focus on the God who gives us the strength to address the demands of life!

Again, before we start breathing out, we first must breathe in! God designed us this way. Just as it is in the physical, so it is in the spiritual! In the natural, we can exhale only so much air before we must breathe in again. So, before we give God a list of our needs, let's first take time to soak in His presence and to inhale His breath of renewal. Why don't you try it right now? Forget for a moment about all of the distractions and needs in your life and begin focusing on how great God is, how much your heavenly Father loves you, and how much He desires to help you in every area of your life. Just breathe in His goodness, His peace, His joy, and His strength. It feels great, doesn't it?

Prayer and Promise Principles

- When we pray, we begin by honoring, worshipping, and praising the Lord simply for who He is.
- When we pray for God's will to be done on earth, we break the spirits of lack, poverty, and insufficiency over our finances, and we release all of God's supernatural provision of abundance and overflow!
- God knows what we need long before we tell Him.
- It's time for you to possess every one of the promises of God!
- The time we invest in worshipping God feeds and replenishes our spirits, souls, and bodies. We "soak up" the Spirit of God, saturating ourselves with His strength, equipping, and anointing. He fills us up so that we can give to others!

Chapter Thirteen

OUR FATHER WHICH ART IN HEAVEN, HALLOWED BE THY NAME

The first key to yoke-destroying, burden-removing, mountain-moving prayers is seen in Jesus' response to the disciples' request for Him to teach them to pray. In Matthew 6:9, He said, *"After this manner therefore pray ye: Our Father which art in heaven, hallowed be thy name."* Now, you and I can repeat that phrase in about two or three seconds, but we're going to take a whole chapter to talk about it because this is truly the foundation of everything in our walks of faith and especially in our prayer lives.

Psalm 100:4 instructs us on how to approach God's throne, saying, *"Enter into his gates with thanksgiving, and into his courts with praise: be thankful unto him, and bless his name."* We gain access to the throne of God through praise, worship, and thanksgiving. Always remember to honor the Lord first before blasting Him with requests, needs, and declarations! Keep in mind that we are coming before a King, and that our manners and protocol count! Our praise carries us into His presence.

Prayer must begin with worship and adoration of God for His immeasurable love, mercy, and goodness. To worship God properly, we need to saturate our thinking with the heart and mind of God by reading His Word. Worship becomes more meaningful and heartfelt when we focus on how incredibly amazing our God is, as well as the incredibly amazing things He wants to do in our lives, which we know from His promises. When you personalize these promises and take ownership of them, a process we

> OUR WORSHIP MOVES TO A HIGHER LEVEL WHEN WE CALL TO MIND THE THINGS THAT THE LORD HAS ALREADY DONE FOR US, FOR THIS ASSURES US OF THE GREAT THINGS HE WILL DO FOR US IN THE FUTURE!

discussed in chapter nine, you will be prompted to worship God continually for His overwhelming goodness, compassion, and mercy.

Praise Him for All His Benefits

Praise the LORD, O my soul, and forget not all his benefits—who forgives all your sins and heals all your diseases, who redeems your life from the pit and crowns you with love and compassion, who satisfies your desires with good things so that your youth is renewed like the eagle's. (Psalm 103:2–5 NIV)

In this passage, the psalmist exhorted himself to "*forget not all his benefits*," and we would do well to exhort ourselves in the same way. In other words, we must keep on reminding ourselves of God's greatness and of the mighty works He has done in our lives. Our worship moves to a higher level when we call to mind the things that the Lord has already done for us, for this assures us of the great things He will do for us in the future! I'm going to go through the names of God in the form of a prayer. This is how I pray, and you can use this as your own guide for worshipful prayer.

Let's Pray!

Father, we thank You for Your presence in our lives. We praise You and worship You for how incredible You are. We are in awe and wonder at how amazing and wonderful You are. We honor You as the Lord of Lords and King of Kings. Thank You for loving us and caring about our lives. Thank You for Your help, Your favor, Your forgiveness, and Your mercy. Thank You for all that You do for us. Thank You that we are on Your mind and in Your heart right now. We praise You for all of Your benefits and for all of Your miraculous help in our lives. We love You, Father. Receive our praises and our love.

Thank You that we are not helpless beggars, but rather that we are Your children, and that You are our loving Father. Fill us with Your love, peace, strength, and joy. We accept and receive Your love for us. Right now, we enter into all that You are and all that You desire to be in our lives.

We thank You that You are:

Jehovah Tsidkenu—You are the Lord who is our righteousness. We are Your temples, and You live within us, changing us from the inside out. Your righteousness is within our own hearts, minds, and spirits, and it's rising up on the insides of us. Every day, You are cleansing us, molding us, shaping us, and causing us to become more like You. Father, create in us clean hearts and renew right spirits within us.

We tap into Your strength to overcome the temptations of the world. We know that greater is He who is in us than he who is in the world. We know that greater is He who is within us than he who is chasing us! Lord, fill our hearts and minds to overflowing with Your thoughts, Your desires, Your nature, and Your compassion. Consume our thoughts with Your thoughts. Replace every bit of our unrighteousness with Your righteousness. We exchange our weaknesses for Your strengths. We thank You that we are more than conquerors through You, and that You have already given us the victory in every area of our lives!

We thank You that You are:

Jehovah M'Kaddesh—You are the God who sanctifies and cleanses us. From glory to glory, You are changing us and shaping us into Your own image. Forgive us for any sins that we have committed and for any evil thoughts that we've entertained. Father, breathe a fresh breath of life into our souls. Give us hearts to serve You and to be lights to the world. We thank You that every morning, Your mercies, grace, and help are fresh and available for us. We exchange our worldly thoughts and ways for Your pure thoughts and ways. Each day, we are renewed in our minds. We thank You that you are never pointing a finger of accusation at us, but that You are reaching out a hand to help us!

We thank You that You are:

Jehovah Shalom—You are the God who fills us with Your peace. In a world of uncertainty and chaos, we draw our peace from You. We find calm and rest in the fact that You love us, and that we are on Your mind right now! We know that You are alert and active, watching over Your Word to perform it. We thank You that You have promised us that no word from heaven will return to You void but will accomplish what You sent it to do. We know that You are going before us, with us, and after us, confirming Your Word in our lives and moving on our behalf. Thank You, Father, that You have ordained for us to have wonderful, abundantly blessed lives. And so, Lord, we step out of the chaos of the world and step into the peace of Your Spirit. Thank You for giving us Your peace, which passes all understanding, in every situation and in all circumstances of our lives!

We thank You that You are:

Jehovah Shammah—You are the God who is wherever we need Him to be, whenever we need Him to be there. We thank You that You are surrounding us with Your divine grace—which is Your boundless ability coming upon us and enabling us to do what we could not otherwise do for ourselves. We thank You that Your favor is surrounding us like a shield, that Your divine favor is helping us, supporting us, assisting us, making our lives and efforts easier, endorsing us, and giving us special advantages and privileges. Thank You for Your supernatural anointing, which is equipping us from the inside out to accomplish all that You have called us to do. You are enduing us with Your abilities, adding Your super to our natural. We know that all things are possible with You. We know that if You are for us, no one can be against us! Father, today we ask You to do a new thing in our lives. Give us a fresh anointing; take the shackles off of our thinking, because we know that You are able to do exceedingly, abundantly above all that we could ask or think! Enlarge our thinking! Enlarge our hearts for You! Enlarge our influence for You! Bless us greatly so that we can be great blessings to others!

We thank You that You are:

Jehovah Rophe—You are the God who heals us. Father, we thank You that You are our Healer if and when we need You to be, and that You have ordained for us to live in divine health. Your name is above every name of sickness and disease. You sent Your Word into the world and healed us. We stand on Your Word and drive out every attack of the enemy and every spirit of sickness or infirmity; we cancel every plan or report of the enemy, and we claim divine health over ourselves, our families, and other loved ones.

Thank You, Father that You heal not only our physical diseases, but our emotional diseases and hurts, as well. Thank You that Jesus was bruised and that He bled to heal us on the inside—to mend our broken hearts and our wounded souls—so that we can live free from burdens, suffering, and pain. Today, Lord, we step out of sickness and disease, and we step into Your divine health and wholeness. We step out of emotional heartbreak, oppression, and depression, and we step into Your divine peace, joy, and contentment. We declare that every form of bondage and every chain is broken off of us forevermore! We are free, free, free, indeed!

We thank You that You are:

Jehovah Nissi—You are the God who is our victory and protection. We know that You have promised us that when the enemy attacks, You will raise up a standard against him. We stand upon Your promise that no weapon formed against us shall prosper. Before we even know that we will face a challenge, You have already worked out a solution! We know that You are making every crooked road straight and every high mountain low! You have promised to go before us, with us, and after us, confirming Your Word with signs, wonders, and miracles. You are our victory in every area of our lives! If You are for us, then who can be against us?

We thank You, Lord, for Your divine protection around our bodies, our minds, and our spirits. We put the blood of Jesus on the doorposts of our homes and on our families, and we declare, "Nothing but the perfect will of God in our homes, our minds, and our families." We release angels to watch over and protect us, and to work on our behalf. We call upon our angels of protection and our angels of destiny. We place a hedge of protection around ourselves, our family members, and other loved ones. We frame our world with the Word of God, and we thank You, Lord, that You are Jehovah Nissi—our victory and our protection—in every area of our lives!

We thank You that You are:

Jehovah Rohi—You are the God who is our shepherd and our guide. We know that the steps of Your righteous men and women are ordered by You. You have promised us that in every place where we put the soles of our feet, You are giving us dominion and authority. We thank You for causing everything to which we put our hands to prosper. We establish in our minds and our lives that You have called us to be the head and not the tail, and that You desire to lead us and promote us into places of authority, dominion, and influence for the furtherance of Your kingdom. Give us Your favor, grace, and anointing to walk into the destinies that You have already planned for us. Open our eyes, our ears, and our minds to God-sized visions for our lives. Help us to enlarge our thinking and to take the limits off of ourselves and off of our perceptions of You. Give us ideas, concepts, insights, innovations, leadership skills, wisdom, and understanding. Give us Your mind, Your heart, and Your discernment to know Your perfect will. Lead us and guide us into all of Your truth, Your ways, and Your destinies for our lives and for our families. Lead us into every one of Your blessings so that we can be great blessings to this world!

We thank You that You are:

Jehovah Jireh—You are the God who is our provider. Father, we praise You that this world and all of its fullness belong to You! We thank You that You have declared in Your Word that it is Your good pleasure to give us, your children, Your kingdom! You created this world and everything in it to be used for Your purposes and to Your glory. You established a covenant of blessing with Your people, and we claim that covenant for our lives! We break every curse of lack, insufficiency, and poverty in the name and by the blood of our Savior, Jesus Christ. We command the spirit of the devourer to be broken over our finances and over our homes! We break every generational curse that would block Your blessings over our lives, our families, and our congregations, as well as over every one of Your children around the world. We command every spirit of poverty and containment over our finances to be shattered forevermore. Every plan of the enemy to steal or even delay our blessings is cancelled and reversed through the authority of Jesus Christ. Every evil report of the enemy is being shredded through the blood of Jesus!

Now, Father, we ask You to release every stored-up blessing that is meant to be in our hands. Every penny that the enemy has ever stolen from us, we call it back with interest! We receive increase, abundance, overflow, promotions, and inheritances. We thank You for Your promise to do exceedingly, abundantly above all that we could even ask, think, or imagine!

Thank You that the windows of heaven are open to us, and that You are rebuking the devourer for our sakes and pouring out blessings so great that we cannot even contain them all, pressed down, shaken together, and running over! Thank You that You are connecting Your super to our natural and bringing supernatural blessing into our lives and through our lives! Thank You that we are not alone, trying to make ends meet, but that You are ready, willing, and able to shower us with abundance and blessings! We praise You that You are watching over Your Word to perform it in our lives!

Thank You that Your very name is **El Shaddai—the God of more than enough!** We receive Your sufficiency and declare it to be so in our lives, every day. In Jesus' name, amen.

We love You, Lord! We give You all the praise, glory, and honor, and we worship You for who You are! We thank You for what You have already done—and what You are going to do—in us, for us, and through us! Hallelujah! Amen!

Didn't that feel great? And we're just getting started!

Prayer and Promise Principles

- We gain access to the throne of God through praise, worship, and thanksgiving. Our praise carries us into His presence.

- Our worship moves to a higher level when we call to mind the things that the Lord has already done for us, for this assures us of the great things He will do for us in the future!

Chapter Fourteen

Thy Kingdom Come. Thy Will Be Done in Earth, as It Is in Heaven

In the last chapter, we established the foundation for all powerful prayer—worship—which is possible only when we know God intimately and understand His nature. This foundation will be the basis for the rest of our discussion about the Lord's Prayer. A deep understanding that God is a good God in every way and at all times is essential, for it will affect and color every part of our lives and futures. It is the firm foundation on which all of our faith and beliefs are built.

Now that we have worshipped God and blessed Him, we are ready to proceed to the second part of the Lord's Prayer: *"Thy kingdom come. Thy will be done in earth, as it is in heaven"* (Matthew 6:10). This is the point where we start boldly declaring the promises of God as found in Scripture. As we pray the promises of God with confidence, we are essentially bringing them to pass in our lives. As we pray the promises, we are prophesying the will of God as expressed through His written Word. Through the power and authority of the name and the blood of our Savior, Jesus, we will tear down the enemy's barriers that are blocking God's blessings from entering our lives. We will break and reverse every curse, generational curses included, that has plagued our lives. We will each put our spiritual foot down and declare, "Nothing but the will of God in my mind, my spirit, my body, my finances, my life, and my future." We will claim this same dominion over our families, churches, schools, cities, states, nations, governments, and even the world.

In establishing this second part of the Lord's Prayer, Jesus authorized us to pray the kingdom of heaven and the will of God into this world. That's a pretty tall order, wouldn't you say? Where do we start, and where do we leave off?

Before we go any further, let me clarify something. Our prayers can be as long, as big, and as far-reaching as we feel led to make them, depending on the times and circumstances. Our primary assignment, though, is to pray for our main spheres of influence. When Jesus prayed to the Father in John 17:9, He said, *"I pray not for the world, but for them which thou hast given me; for they are thine."* Even Jesus, the Savior of the world, focused His prayers and energies on His primary circle of influence. So it is with us. Our main focus in prayer is to be within our own spheres of influence. Granted, Jesus' circle of influence was much larger than any of ours—it included all the chosen ones, those who would accept Him as their Lord and Savior.

> THE LORD DOESN'T EXPECT US TO FEEL AN OVERWHELMING, HEAVY BURDEN OR A PERSONAL RESPONSIBILITY FOR EVERY SINGLE SPECIFIC SOUL IN EVERY CORNER OF THE WORLD AT EVERY MOMENT OF EVERY DAY.

The Lord doesn't expect us to feel an overwhelming, heavy burden or a personal responsibility for every single specific soul in every corner of the world at every moment of every day. After all, it's impossible for us, as finite beings with extremely limited knowledge, to know about and pray for all of the members of our *communities*, let alone our *world!*

There have been stages in my past when I felt that I wasn't doing enough—wasn't praying enough, wasn't witnessing enough, wasn't feeling a heavy enough burden for souls. But I have finally come to realize that the Lord never intended for us to live under a blanket of spiritual heaviness, sadness, or self-condemnation. Our Father doesn't drive us with guilt; He motivates us with compassion. My goal is the same: I don't want us to feel *driven* to pray; I want us to feel *motivated* to pray!

Nothing but the Will of God on Earth, as It Is in Heaven

"Thy kingdom come. Thy will be done in earth, as it is in heaven." God has given you and me the authority through prayer to establish God's will on earth, just as it is established to prevail in heaven.

Since most of us have not been to heaven, we need to paint a general picture for ourselves of what it will be like, based on God's Word. Is there any sickness or disease in heaven? Is there any poverty or lack in heaven? Is there any depression or sadness? Any fear? Any doubt? Any sin or rebellion? Any confusion, chaos, or strife? No, of course not! Heaven is a place that is full of only the wonderful goodness and blessings of God! It is filled with joy, happiness, peace, wholeness, abundance, and overflow! Nothing but the will of God exists in heaven. So, through our prayers, we are to establish that nothing but the will of God exists on earth, either!

> NOTHING BUT THE WILL OF GOD EXISTS IN HEAVEN. SO, THROUGH OUR PRAYERS, WE ARE TO ESTABLISH THAT NOTHING BUT THE WILL OF GOD EXISTS ON EARTH, EITHER!

Jesus is instructing us to take authority over all of the enemy's dominion on earth, spiritually and physically, and to establish the dominion of God, just as it is established in heaven. We are authorized to literally bring heaven to earth. If it's not allowed in God's kingdom in heaven, it's not going to be allowed in His kingdom on earth. Nothing but the good and perfect will of God!

It's exhilarating to realize the authority, dominion, and power that the Lord has entrusted to us! It's also incredibly exciting to realize that we don't have to live with or accept all of the challenges and circumstances that are thrown our way. Through the power entrusted to us, we can pray and change the course of the world! Again, rather than telling our God how big our problems are, we're going to be telling our problems how big our God is!

Take It by Force

The process of praying the kingdom of God on earth is never performed without resistance by the enemy. Our heavenly Father isn't the only one with a plan for our lives—Satan plots schemes of his own that he hopes we'll follow, instead. But prayer gives us the opportunity to rebuke, destroy, and shred the plans that he has for us. I like to picture in my mind an actual document shredder. As I pray against the devil's plans, I visualize myself putting his plans through the shredder and seeing them torn into pieces that are impossible to put back together!

Matthew 11:12 says, *"From the days of John the Baptist until now, the kingdom of heaven has been forcefully advancing, and forceful men lay hold of it"* (NIV). To be forceful in advancing the kingdom of heaven, we must put on the full armor of God, which Paul described in the book of Ephesians. He said,

> *Be strong in the Lord, and in the power of his might. Put on the whole armour of God, that ye may be able to stand against the wiles of the devil. For we wrestle not against flesh and blood, but against principalities, against powers, against the rulers of the darkness of this world, against spiritual wickedness in high places. Wherefore take unto you the whole armour of God, that ye may be able to withstand in the evil day, and having done all, to stand.* (Ephesians 6:10–13)

Paul picked up the same topic in 2 Corinthians 10:4, saying, *"The weapons we fight with are not the weapons of the world. On the contrary, they have divine power to demolish strongholds"* (NIV). Armed with the spiritual weaponry of God, we can defeat the devil and keep his kingdom from reigning on earth.

Recognizing the Enemy's Cunning Schemes

I don't want to give the devil too much credit, but I also don't want to underestimate the extent of his insidious influence, nor the effectiveness of his cunning wiles. His job is to steal, kill, and destroy. (See John 10:10.) He is a liar and a deceiver; he is the accuser of the brethren. He hates God, and he hates God's people. We don't need to fear him, but we do need to recognize him and be wary of his schemes. He's been at his profession for a very long time, and he is extremely skilled in his craft of manipulation and deception.

Doubt

The oldest trick in his book is to cause us to doubt God and His Word. Remember what he spoke to Eve in the garden of Eden to tempt her to eat the forbidden fruit? He said,

> *Has God indeed said, "You shall not eat of every tree of the garden"?… You will not surely die. For God knows that in the day you eat of it your eyes will be opened, and you will be like God, knowing good and evil.*
> (Genesis 3:1, 4–5 NKJV)

Nothing delights Satan more than causing us to doubt the One he hates the most—God. If he can discredit God's authority and power in our eyes, minds, and hearts, he can block the flow of the Lord's miracle-working power from our lives. We can't afford to be deceived!

Fear

Another one of the devil's favorite tactics is to create and feed the spirit of fear, especially within Christian believers. Think about what Americans learned about the strategies of world terrorists after 9/11. These terrorists didn't use advanced military weapons like those in the arsenals of most developed countries. They didn't even have a significant amount of man-power. For these reasons, the fear they inspired in the hearts of American citizens—and citizens across the world—was probably even greater than it would have been had they armed themselves with cutting-edge weaponry and assembled themselves in a large company. The fact that a few men with limited resources managed to take so many lives and cause such great destruction—something no one could have expected—planted widespread fear and terror in the hearts of the people they considered their enemies.

While the events of 9/11 caused immediate destruction and death, the fear that has lingered since then has been perhaps even more devastating, and it threatens to topple more than just skyscrapers. The fear of what might occur wreaked havoc in almost every person, corporation, and institution in our country. We became terrorized by the fear of the unknown. Our nation was nearly paralyzed by the threat of another attack, not knowing when, where, or how it would happen.

THE TRUTH IS, SATAN HAS NO REAL POWER OR AUTHORITY UNLESS WE FORFEIT THE DOMINION THAT GOD HAS GIVEN US. THE ONLY DOMINION THE DEVIL REALLY HAS IS THE DOMINION THAT WE ALLOW HIM TO TAKE.

The enemy of our souls works much like a terrorist. First Peter 5:8 describes him like this: *"Your enemy the devil prowls around like a roaring lion looking for someone to devour"* (NIV). The truth is, Satan has no real power or authority unless we forfeit the dominion that God has given us. The only dominion the devil really has is the dominion that we allow him to take. As James 4:7 tells us, *"Submit yourselves therefore to God. Resist the devil, and he will flee from you."*

We Are More than Conquerors!

First John 4:4 assures us that *"the one who is in you is greater than the one who is in the world"* (NIV). The One who is in us is almighty God! That means that you and I have more power in our pinkies than the devil and all his forces have in the entire universe! We don't ever need to fear the devil, for his power was defeated by Jesus at the cross!

Larry deals specifically with this truth in his book *Free at Last*. In a chapter called "Jesus' Feet Won Back Dominion over the Places We Walk," he explains,

> Jesus shed His blood...where they drove the spikes through His feet, nailing Him to the cross. The blood shed from His feet also redeemed us from our loss of dominion and authority. Man was supposed to be the head and not the tail. (See Deuteronomy 28:13.) That is our place through the shed blood of Jesus. When Adam disobeyed God in the garden of Eden, he lost dominion and authority, and at that moment, Satan became the god of this world. But through Jesus' shed blood, we don't have to be trampled by Satan. Instead, we are to trample him!

Every place on which the sole of your foot treads shall be yours.
(Deuteronomy 11:24 NKJV)

We have been commanded to *"go into all the world and preach the good news to all creation"* (Mark 16:15 NIV). Wherever we go, we're to tell people, *"The kingdom of God is near. Repent and believe the good news!"* (Mark 1:15 NIV). This would be impossible unless we had the authority to take dominion over Satan's earthly kingdom. We are told to *"be strong and courageous. Do not be afraid or terrified...for the LORD your God goes with you; he will never leave you nor forsake you"* (Deuteronomy 31:6 NIV). Dominion over this earth is ours again because of the shed blood of Jesus Christ, and wherever we are, the kingdom of heaven is at hand.[5]

The enemy's schemes and strategies are never meant to overcome us; we are meant to overcome them through the blood of the Lamb! Always remember that *"we are more than conquerors through him that loved us"* (Romans 8:37)! We should never let the devil back us into a corner where we cower in fear.

Let me paint another picture for you. Larry and I have a wonderful Rottweiler named Harley, and he has been specially trained to protect our family (mainly my daughter Katie and me) as a guard dog. Whenever Harley is off duty, however, he thinks he's a lap dog—and he weighs a massive 115 pounds! With no reservations and without forewarning, he'll climb right up on Larry's lap as if he were a tiny cocker spaniel.

There are times, though, when he becomes somewhat overprotective of Katie or me for no apparent reason. I might be standing in the kitchen talking to someone, and Harley will suddenly back into me and try to push me away from the other person. If I submit to his defensive agenda, he'll have me backed into a corner at the far end of the house in no time at all! The dog trainer told me that I have to maintain authority over Harley and continually make him understand that I'm the boss. I'm the human; he's the dog. If I don't take a dominant stand over him, he will take a dominant stand over me. So, I have had to learn to continue to keep him in his place, even if it bruises his tender feelings. Don't worry—we always kiss and make up!

[5] Huch, *Free at Last*, 151–152.

This is exactly how the devil will work in our lives—if we let him. He'll back us into a corner, dominate us, and intimidate us. Just like my trainer told me to do with Harley, we need to show the devil who's boss! Put your foot down! Put him in his rightful place—under your feet! Don't let him bully you or push you around. Stand your spiritual ground and drive him out! Send him home, crying like a little sissy! Stand strong in the authority and dominion that God has placed within you. As Paul said, *"Fight the good fight of faith"* (1 Timothy 6:12).

Muzzle Satan with the Word of God

> WHEN WE START WITH THE WORD, WE START WITH THE ANSWER TO EVERY QUESTION, THE SOLUTION TO EVERY PROBLEM, AND THE AUTHORITY OVER EVERYTHING ON THE EARTH AND IN HEAVEN.

When Satan tempted Jesus in the wilderness, Jesus withstood his enticements by relying on the Word of God. Each time, He responded, *"It is written…"* (Matthew 4:4, 6, 10). He defeated Satan with the Word of God, and that's exactly what we need to do. When we start with the Word, we start with the answer to every question, the solution to every problem, and the authority over everything on the earth and in heaven. Satan has no defense or weapon that stands a chance against the Word of God, which is *"sharper than any twoedged sword"* (Hebrews 4:12).

When we confess the Word—which is the will of God—aloud, it nullifies the power of the enemy. When he whispers negative thoughts into our minds, we need to talk right back to him and override his threats with the promises of God. Silence him! Muzzle him! Stick a spiritual sock in his mouth! When that whirlpool of negative thoughts tries to take you down, reverse it! Create an upward whirlpool with the positive promises of God. Speak them out loud!

Your mind cannot retain a negative thought when you speak a positive thought aloud. Our spoken words will always override our silent thoughts. Therefore, when we pray, let's pray out loud so that we're heard loud and clear by the devil, as well as by our God and our own spirits. Let it be heard far and wide, *"We are more than conquerors through him that loved us!"*

Now that we're all fired up to pray, let's actually pray! This is how we'll pray through the second part of the Lord's Prayer: *"Thy kingdom come. Thy will be done in earth, as it is in heaven"* (Matthew 6:10).

Let's Pray!

Father, we thank You for Your love and for Your presence in our lives. Thank You for Your Word. Thank You that You have entrusted us with Your authority and dominion in every area of our lives, our families, and our futures. Right now, we declare, *"Thy kingdom come. Thy will be done in earth, as it is in heaven."* In the name and by the blood of Jesus, we claim nothing but the will of God in our lives! It's not by our own might or power but by Your Spirit that we will be victorious in every area. You have called us to be more than conquerors. We know that in heaven, Your perfect will prevails. There is no sickness, no disease, no oppression, no sin, no addictions, and no strife or turmoil in heaven. And so we claim the same things in this life—in ourselves, in our families, in our homes, and in our futures. Father, we declare Your liberty, freedom, joy, victory, and dominion!

Today, we are framing our world with the Word of God. We thank You for the promise in James 5:16 that *"the effectual fervent prayer of a righteous man* [or woman] *availeth much"*—it has great power. Father, You are not a reluctant, faraway, indifferent God. You are a loving, generous Father who cares for and loves us deeply. We don't come as beggars or strangers, but we come as Your children, joint-heirs with Jesus Christ. Thank You for giving us the keys to the kingdom. Whatever we bind on earth will be bound in heaven, and whatever we loose on earth will be loosed in heaven. We are not begging You to help us; we are simply entering into what You have already done for us. We are appropriating Your nature into our hearts. We are releasing and stepping into the promises in Your Word.

You have empowered us and enabled us to establish Your dominion in every area of our minds, hearts, bodies, and lives. We command that every attack or stronghold of the enemy be broken. We speak divine peace and joy over our minds and over the minds of our spouses, our children, our other family members, and our other loved ones. We declare nothing but the will of God and the mind of God. We break every spirit that would try to tempt us or torment us, and we release Your faith, strength, and will in every area of our lives. We send every deceiving, lying, scheming spirit back to the pit of hell, and we receive the peace, direction, and light of Your Word into our hearts. We break every curse of sickness and disease, and we release divine health and long life upon us. We tear down every stronghold of fear, doubt, anxiety, and unbelief that would try to grip our minds. We replace them with the faith, hope, and vision of the promises of our God.

Thank You, Father, that You have given us authority over all the power of the enemy. So, we put our feet down and boldly declare, "Nothing but the perfect will of God in our families and in our households." We drive out every spirit of strife, division, discord, and rebellion, and we release the spirit of unity, harmony, and peace. We command anger, resentment, bitterness, and sorrow to leave forevermore. We choose to fill our hearts and our homes with love, joy, happiness, forgiveness, and wholeness. All of the blessings that are present in heaven are going to be present in this world and in our households.

Father, we bind every spirit of darkness that would try to attack our families. We bind every spirit that would try to lay hold of our children. We rebuke every ungodly influence in their lives. We plead the blood of Jesus Christ on the doorposts of their minds. Father, we call them home to a relationship with You. We call them into Your perfect will. Nothing but Your perfect will be done in their lives. We declare the righteousness of God to rule and reign in their hearts and lives. Father, we pray that You would send godly influences into their lives. Raise them up to be leaders in Your kingdom. Raise them up to be men and women after Your own heart. We speak righteousness into their hearts and minds. Let Your blessing and anointing flow into them and through them. Father, create a hedge of protection around their minds. We plead the blood of Jesus on them, and we claim them for Your kingdom. As for me and my house, we will serve the Lord! We give You praise for it, Lord. Hallelujah!

Father, we thank You that in John 10:10, You have said that You came to give us life, and that life more abundantly—full of glory, joy, peace, victory, and abundance! We speak that fullness and wholeness into every area of our lives: our homes, our marriages, our families, and so forth. We claim Romans 8:37: You have called us to be more than conquerors. No matter what circumstances we're facing, You have called us and equipped us to be victorious conquerors.

You have promised us in Romans 8:28 that all things work together for the good of those who love You. So, Father, no matter what the enemy has dished out to us in the past, no matter what circumstances we have faced, You will take every attack of the enemy and turn it into something wonderful. You will weave all the details and experiences of our lives into beautiful tapestries.

Father, we thank You for the assurance in Colossians 3:3–4 in that the Lord Himself *has* our lives and that the Lord Himself *is* our life. I pray that the life, liberty, and joy of God would rise up on the insides of us.

Lord, we know that You desire, design, and destine us to win and be successful in every area of our lives. Lead us into Your perfect plans, designs, and destinies. Thank You that we are living under an open heaven and that we are entering into every promise that You have placed in Your Book. We take personal ownership of these promises, and we thank You in advance for fulfilling them in our lives. Father, we pray that You would release all of those promises into us, for us, and through us.

We thank You for Your divine protection—physical, spiritual, and emotional—over us, our families, our spouses, our children, and our friends. Father, fill us with Your wisdom, Your insight, and Your understanding. Your Word says that the steps of righteous men and women are ordered by the Lord, so we ask that You would go before us, with us, and after us, releasing Your will and Your blessings in our lives. Father, we ask You to make every high mountain low and every crooked path straight. We thank You that Jesus Christ Himself triumphed over Satan and defeated him in every area—past, present, and future. And so, today, we claim Matthew 6:10: *"Thy will be done"* in our lives. Nothing but the will of God.

Father, we thank You that in Deuteronomy 1:30, You have given us the promise that You will go before us and fight for us. Thank You, too, for the promise of Deuteronomy 3:22: *"Ye shall not fear… for the Lord your God he shall fight for you."* We claim the promise of Psalm 5:12 that the favor of God will surround us and our families like a shield, as well as the promise of Psalm 138:7–8 that the Lord will preserve our lives and never abandon us.

We rebuke every spirit of poverty, lack, and insufficiency. We break every generational curse of failure. We put our feet on the neck of the enemy. We place the blood of Jesus over our finances and our futures. We drive out every attack and silence the voice of the enemy. Through the blood of Jesus Christ, we cancel and shred every one of his plans for our lives! Every spirit of containment is shattered. Every generational curse of poverty, toil, and struggle is canceled today, tomorrow, and forevermore!

Now, Lord, we release all of Your plans and blessings into our lives. We claim every generational blessing of prosperity, abundance, increase, and overflow! We call in the blessings and the promises of our God! We speak divine favor, grace, and anointing over everything that we put our hands to. We speak dominion on every place where we put the soles of our feet. We claim every single dollar that is meant to be in our hands to build the kingdom of God, to bless Your people, and to bless our own lives and families. We thank You that it is Your good pleasure to give us the kingdom, and also that You are applying Your super to our natural, creating supernatural blessing in every area of our lives!

We thank You for Your divine mercy, grace, favor, and equipping. Your favor is supporting us, assisting us, making our lives easier, and giving us special advantages and privileges. You are equipping us from the inside out to do all that You have called us to do. Your grace is enabling us to do what we never could have done on our own.

Father, we thank You for Your anointing, which is enduing us with Your supernatural abilities. We are not living under the circumstances and restrictions of this natural world. Instead, we are stepping into Your supernatural realm of help, supply, equipping, and miraculous provision—and we praise You for it!

Father, we thank You that You watch over Your Word to perform it, and that Your Word will not return to You void but will accomplish that which You sent it out to do. You will not drop the work that You have begun in our lives. We claim Psalm 92:13–14, which tells us that those who are *"planted in the house of the* LORD... *will flourish in the courts of our God. They will still bear fruit in old age, they will stay fresh and green"* (NIV). Lord, we thank You that we are filled with Your strength, health, nourishment, help, vitality, long life, happiness, growth, and productivity. Psalm 144:15 promises us, *"Happy is that people, whose God is the* LORD.*"* Hallelujah!

And Lord, we stand in the gap for our families, our neighborhoods, our schools, our churches, our cities, our nation, and for all the other nations of the world. Release Your will. Through the blood of Jesus Christ, we drive back every force of darkness that's encroaching on this world. Draw hearts and souls back to You. Father, draw our nations back to You. Father, draw our schools and our children back to You. Capture the hearts of the children of this nation and of this world for You, Lord. We claim, *"Thy will be done in earth, as it is in heaven."* Nothing but the will of God!

Now, Father, we give You praise that Your will, Your purposes, and Your plans are being accomplished in our lives and in the world. We thank You for giving us complete and total victory in every area and for working Your Word in us, for us, and through us. Father, bless us greatly so that we can be great blessings to others, in Jesus' name.

Thank You that we are possessing the promises of our God! Amen!

Now, shout "Hallelujah!" and seal it all with some praise and thanksgiving! Hallelujah!

Prayer and Promise Principles

* We proclaim, "Nothing but the will of God in our minds, our spirits, our bodies, our finances, our lives, and our futures!"

* Jesus authorized us to pray the kingdom of heaven and the will of God into this world.

* Nothing but the will of God exists in heaven. So, through our prayers, we are to establish that nothing but the will of God exists on earth, either!

* The enemy's schemes and strategies are never meant to overcome us; we are meant to overcome them through the blood of the Lamb!

* When the enemy whispers negative thoughts into our minds, we need to talk right back to him and override his threats with the promises of God. Silence him! Muzzle him! Stick a spiritual sock in his mouth!

* Jesus Christ defeated Satan with the Word of God, and that's exactly what we need to do. When we start with the Word, we start with the answer to every question, the solution to every problem, and the authority over everything on the earth and in heaven.

Chapter Fifteen

GIVE US THIS DAY OUR DAILY BREAD

When I teach about this portion of the Lord's Prayer, people often ask me, "Doesn't the term *our daily bread* mean that God will give us a daily word to sustain us and give us hope?" Many Scripture verses have multiple implications and can speak to us on many levels. This specific part of the Lord's Prayer, however, is speaking about God's literal supply of provision to meet our daily needs. It has never been God's intention for His children to live in lack or poverty.

Our God is a loving, kind, benevolent Father who has made provision in every area of our lives to help and assist us. Through prayer, we are able to approach His throne of grace, mercy, and favor to obtain help in times of need. This open door of assistance includes our financial needs in addition to all of our other needs. The Lord has given you and me—His children—special privilege and access to His supernatural, limitless supply.

Many people have a tendency to "spiritualize" the terms used in the Bible, interpreting such terms as *blessing, grace,* and *favor* as vague, abstract words, albeit lofty and nice-sounding ones. The Bible is filled with warnings about the allure of money, most of which can be summarized by 1 Timothy 6:10: *"For the love of money is a root of all kinds of evil"* (NIV).

Too often, though, we mistake these warnings for a condemnation of prosperity, and we attach negative connotations to money and wealth. We feel guilty about asking the Lord for money, fearing that it's *"filthy lucre"* [*"dishonest gain"* NIV] (see 1 Timothy 3:3, 8; Titus 1:7; 1 Peter 5:2).

But I am absolutely convinced—and I hope to convince you—that our Father is not the least bit insulted when we talk to Him about money! We must clarify and grasp what the Lord really promises us in the area of finances.

Money Is an Amplifier

The Bible doesn't say that money is the root of all evil; it says that the *love* of money is the root of all *kinds* of evil. Money, in and of itself, is not evil. Rather, money is a positive thing—it's an amplifier of blessings! In the hands of evil or ungodly people, money becomes a means to further the malicious plans in their hearts. But in the hands of good, godly people, money becomes a means to build God's kingdom and bless His people on earth! Money is a tool that is used to accomplish the desires of him who possesses it. Of course, we have all seen lives, businesses, and churches harmed and even destroyed by greed and the abuse of money. But, I have seen just as much, if not more, destruction that was caused by the effects of poverty, debt, and hopelessness!

> MONEY, IN AND OF ITSELF, IS NOT EVIL. RATHER, MONEY IS A POSITIVE THING—IT'S AN AMPLIFIER OF BLESSINGS!

At creation, God made a beautiful, abundant world that He intended for His children to enjoy. He certainly didn't go to all the effort of creating a magnificent world for the devil's crowd, right? In Genesis, God created Adam and Eve, blessed them, told them to be fruitful and to multiply, and gave them dominion over all animals, insects, plants, and natural resources of the earth. In Genesis 2:11, He instructed them where to find gold, and then in verse 12, He added, *"And the gold of that land is good."* Did you catch that? God Himself pointed out to Adam and Eve where they could find gold, then went on to tell them that it was *good!* He didn't say that it was evil or that it would lead to their destruction, poison their hearts, or cause the downfall of civilization. In fact, He went on to point out to them other precious metals and stones—several of the wonderful things He created for their needs and pleasures.

The warning is not to avoid money and material things but to avoid placing too much importance on these things. You may have heard the saying, "God wants us to have things; He just doesn't want things to have us." I like to say it like this: "God isn't asking us to take a vow of *poverty*, but He is asking us to take a vow of *priorities*." It has always been God's plan and desire to bless His people with wealth, influence, and dominion. And that includes—in fact, it requires—financial blessings! The key to living in *His* realm of blessings is keeping *Him* as the number one priority of our lives—not just in theory, but in reality!

The Lord Takes Pleasure in the Prosperity of His Servants

Psalm 35:27 says, "*Let the* LORD *be magnified, which hath pleasure in the prosperity of his servant.*" Prosperity encompasses wholeness, completeness, well-being, and peace. Some people might argue that this verse isn't speaking about financial prosperity. Let's forget about doctrine for a minute and just talk common sense. It is impossible to be in a state of completeness, wholeness, well-being, and peace when the bill collectors are chasing you down and threatening to cancel your phone service, impound your car, or evict you from your home! It's anything but peaceful when your children need school supplies, clothes, and medicine, and your checkbook balance is zero!

It is preposterous and illogical to think that financial blessings are excluded from the package deal that God has for us. I believe that God not only sees and cares about the enormous financial burdens that we live under, but that He also has a specific plan to free us from those burdens! He has promised to release upon us the burden-removing, yoke-destroying power of God. Debt is a burden—one that God removes!

We've all witnessed the destructive force of poverty in nations around the world, and perhaps even in our own communities. Our hearts go out to those who are suffering from the results of severe poverty. But the burden of not being able to make ends meet affects most of us at some point or another. It's not pretty; it's not pleasant. And it's not God's will!

Again, we know that our God is a good God by understanding His names, especially Jehovah Jireh—our Provider—and El Shaddai—our God of more than enough.

I know that God has a desire and a plan for you and me to move out of the realm of lack and into His realm of provision; to move from "not enough" into "more than enough"; to break the burden of insufficiency and release the spirit of overflow and abundance!

His name is Jehovah Jireh—our Provider! His name is El Shaddai—the God of more than enough! Remember, these names aren't just random tags He chose for Himself. Rather, His names are intentional, significant identifiers that describe His nature, His heart, and His desires. They convey who He wants to be for us and what He wants to do in our lives!

PROSPERITY, WEALTH, DOMINION, AND INFLUENCE WERE PART OF GOD'S PLAN FOR MANKIND FROM THE VERY BEGINNING!

In Deuteronomy 8:18, we read, *"But thou shalt remember the LORD thy God: for it is he that giveth thee power to get wealth, that he may establish his covenant which he sware unto thy fathers, as it is this day."* We see from this verse that wealth—and the pursuit thereof—is not a man-made idea but rather something that God Himself initiated. Prosperity, wealth, dominion, and influence were part of God's plan for mankind from the very beginning!

The depictions of prosperity as something inherently evil and ungodly, and poverty as something inherently good and godly, cannot be found in the Bible. Proverbs 10:22 says, *"The blessing of the LORD brings wealth, and he adds no trouble to it"* (NIV).

In other words, there is a wealth that will bring sorrow with it if it has been gained through ungodly means. But wealth that is gained through godly means brings great blessings with no strings attached.

Allow me to reemphasize that it's all about priorities. Whether we are wealthy or impoverished or anything in between, we must keep the Lord as the center of all that we do and honor Him with our firstfruits, tithes, and offerings. When we truly put Him first and do our best to obey His Word, He will honor His promises and bless everything we put our hands to.

God's Covenant of Blessing

As we've said, God has made a covenant of blessing with His people. This covenant consists of two parts: God's part and our part. At this point, we need to talk about the basic requirements to move forward into the supernatural financial blessings of God. I absolutely am convinced that the Lord wants us to take Him at His word and to claim His promises with bold faith. However, I certainly don't want to give the impression that God is a puppet on a string. The blessings of God are part of His package deal. God has made a covenant of blessing with His people—a contract.

As we know, a contract is made between two parties, each of whom has a responsibility to uphold his end of the bargain.

In Deuteronomy 8, God laid out some of the specific terms of His covenant to the new generation. The children of Israel had been wandering in the wilderness for forty years because of their disobedience and unbelief, but now they were about to enter the Promised Land.

Sometimes, our own lives seem to be on hold; we find ourselves "wandering in the wilderness" because of our lack of obedience and faith. I think we would all agree that wandering in circles and getting nowhere in the wilderness is not a fun place to be!

Keeping God First in Our Lives Releases His Blessings, Abundance, and Overflow

In order to release the blessings of God, we must walk in obedience to His commandment to love, honor, and worship Him.

I want you to read the following Scriptures because they lay out so clearly how immensely the Lord wants to bless us and to establish His dominion and His covenant through us. Then, just as clearly, He lays out the requirements on our part. It's a win-win situation for us! This understanding is the essential key to getting our prayers answered, our miracles released, and our lives supernaturally blessed!

Be careful to follow every command I am giving you today, so that you may live and increase and may enter and possess the land that the LORD promised on oath to your forefathers. Remember how the LORD your God led you all the way in the desert these forty years, to humble you and to test you in order to know what was in your heart, whether or not you would keep his commands. (Deuteronomy 8:1–2 NIV)

We see here that the Israelites' double-mindedness and lack of commitment to the Lord prolonged their journey by forty years. The journey should have taken only a short period of time, but until the Israelites got their hearts right, God kept saying, in essence, "Okay, kids—take another lap!" Just as it is with us, their rebellion and spiritual laxity only prolonged the agony and pain. In hindsight, they probably said, "What were we thinking?" Let's learn from their mistakes so that we can "fast-forward" to the good stuff in our own lives!

Verses 6–18 go on to admonish them,

Observe the commands of the LORD your God, walking in his ways and revering him. For the LORD your God is bringing you into a good land—a land with streams and pools of water, with springs flowing in the valleys and hills; a land with wheat and barley, vines and fig trees, pomegranates, olive oil and honey; a land where bread will not be scarce and you will lack nothing; a land where the rocks are iron and you can dig copper out of the hills. When you have eaten and are satisfied, praise the LORD your God for the good land he has given you. Be careful that you do not forget the LORD your God, failing to observe his commands, his laws and his decrees that I am giving you this day. Otherwise, when you eat and are satisfied, when you build fine houses and settle down, and when your herds and flocks grow large and your silver and gold increase and all you have is multiplied, then your heart will become proud and you will forget the LORD your God, who brought you out of Egypt, out of the land of slavery. He led you through the vast and dreadful desert, that thirsty and waterless land, with its venomous snakes and scorpions. He brought you water out of hard rock. He gave you manna to eat in the desert, something your fathers had never known, to humble and to test you so that in the end it might go well with you. You may say to yourself, "My power and the strength of my hands have produced this wealth for me." But remember the LORD *your God, for it is he who gives you the ability to produce wealth, and so confirms his covenant, which he swore to your forefathers, as it is today.* (NIV)

The important point to see here is that we always need to keep God first in every area of our lives, for any blessings or good fortune we experience come from Him. It's easy to remember God when we're in distress, but we often forget Him when everything seems to be going our way, and we mistakenly credit our own abilities and skills instead of God's provision and blessing. As Paul wrote in 1 Corinthians 4:7, *"What do you have that you did not receive? And if you did receive it, why do you boast as if you did not?"* (NIV).

God desires to bless us and bring us into a good land—a good place with abundance and plentiful resources and blessings. It is His will to multiply everything we put our hands to, as well as to establish His covenant in us, for us, and through us. However, we must heed the warning from Deuteronomy and keep our part of the covenant if we expect God to keep His part.

> GOD DESIRES TO BLESS US AND BRING US INTO A GOOD LAND— A GOOD PLACE WITH ABUNDANCE AND PLENTIFUL RESOURCES AND BLESSINGS. HOWEVER, WE MUST HEED THE WARNING FROM DEUTERONOMY AND KEEP OUR PART OF THE COVENANT IF WE EXPECT GOD TO KEEP HIS PART.

We need to keep God first—not just in *theory* but in *actuality*.

The commandment *"to fear him"* (Deuteronomy 8:6) has several implications. First of all, it means recognizing His holiness, righteousness, and justice, as well as His mercy, grace, and favor. He is a holy God whose very nature causes Him to judge sin, unrighteousness, and disobedience. We can never take Him for granted or disrespect Him. He is worthy of all of our praise, all of our hearts, and all of our lives!

Always Hold the Lord in a Place of Honor, Respect, Wonder, and Awe

Second, the commandment to "*fear him*" means to hold Him in high regard and esteem, to view Him with reverence, honor, wonder, and awe. We need to respect and recognize the greatness, power, righteousness, goodness, and majesty of our God! One way of thinking of the term *fear* when it relates to God is to regard Him with awe and wonder and experience the so-called wow factor.

Picture a young child on her first trip to Disney World. One glance at Cinderella's Castle and she is awestruck, mouth hanging wide open in amazement. How much more awestruck should our response be to the all-powerful God? He is absolutely amazing, incredible, and majestic beyond description, and He loves us with an everlasting love. He wants to have an intimate relationship with each of us; but let's never take this incredible privilege for granted. Let's always treat Him with the respect, honor, and awe that He deserves!

Tithing: Another Divine Exchange

Tithing and giving cause God to throw open the floodgates of heaven and shower us with His blessings. One of His commandments that we need to keep in order to release His blessings is found in Malachi 3:10, where God directed us to honor Him with our firstfruits, tithes, and offerings.

> "*Bring the whole tithe into the storehouse, that there may be food in my house. Test me in this," says the LORD Almighty, "and see if I will not throw open the floodgates of heaven and pour out so much blessing that you will not have room enough for it.*" (NIV)

Parting with our hard-earned money is not something we're naturally inclined to do. Giving to God is a choice that we make by faith as we trust His promise to provide for our needs. We've already talked about prayer being a divine exchange, and tithing—giving God 10 percent of our earnings—is also a divine exchange. We give Him our tithes and offerings; in exchange, He throws open the floodgates of heaven and pours out so much blessing that we can't even hold it all! Every dollar we give to God's work,

He promises to multiply back to us. The more we give, the more He gives back to us. That is by far the best return we could ever find on our investments. That is a great deal!

God Isn't after Our Money; He's after Our Hearts

Giving really isn't about the dollar amount; rather, it's about our obedience, our love for God above our love for possessions and wealth, and our faith and trust that He is a God who keeps His word. God isn't after our money; He's after our hearts. Let me assure you of this: we can never over-trust Him, and we can never out-give Him. In the words of Thomas Aquinas, "God is no one's debtor."[6] God owes us nothing, and yet He gives us everything! As we read in Romans 11:35–36, *"Who has ever given to God, that God should repay him? For from him and through him and to him are all things"* (NIV).

> THE MORE WE GIVE, THE MORE GOD GIVES BACK TO US.

Our giving is what opens the supernatural outpouring of God's financial blessings. Our obedience is the foundation that gives us the right to pray and call upon Him, claiming the blessings that He has promised us in His Word. Once we have established this habit of tithing and giving, we're promised that God will provide. Read the following Scriptures about finances:

Humility and the fear of the LORD bring wealth and honor and life.
(Proverbs 22:4 NIV)

Every man also to whom God has given wealth and possessions and power to enjoy them, and to accept his lot and find enjoyment in his toil—this is the gift of God. (Ecclesiastes 5:19 RSV)

If you will only let me help you, if you will only obey, then I will make you rich! (Isaiah 1:19 TLB)

---

[6] Thomas Aquinas, *Summa Theologica*, First Part of the Second Part–Question 114. Trans. Fathers of the English Dominican Province, 1947. New Advent, Inc. http://history.hanover.edu/courses/excerpts/346ta2.html.

Thus says the LORD, your Redeemer, the Holy One of Israel: I am the LORD your God, who teaches you to profit, who leads you in the way you should go. (Isaiah 48:17 RSV)

My God shall supply all your need according to his riches in glory by Christ Jesus. (Philippians 4:19)

Beloved, I pray that you may prosper in all things and be in health, just as your soul prospers. (3 John 1:2 NKJV)

The Promises That We Take Ownership of Will Change Our Circumstances and Our Lives

I think it is quite evident from the above Scriptures alone that it is truly God's will and desire to bless His people in every way and in every area of their lives. I felt it necessary to lay a foundation and to break away any misgivings or misinformation that would try to block us from receiving all that God has for us. The Word tells us, *"For as* [a man] *thinks in his heart, so is he"* (Proverbs 23:7 NKJV). If we feel guilty about being blessed or about asking God to bless us financially, then we will literally reject the miracles that God is trying to send. Remember, it's the truth we *know* that sets us free! It's the promises we take ownership of that will change our circumstances and our lives.

How about praying that God will move on our behalf and connect us to our miracles before we need the prayer for rescue? You may have heard the maxim, "closing the barn door after the horse has already fled." Well, that's how a lot of people view prayer. They pray only *after* a crisis occurs! I'm talking about praying and appropriating God's provision *before* a crisis occurs.

Instead of trying to chase down your miracles, you'll have miracles chasing you. There will always be times when we need God to *sustain* us through certain circumstances, but prayer is also meant to miraculously *change* our circumstances!

Not only does God want to meet our daily needs, but He is also looking for faithful people through whom He can pour great amounts of wealth! There is going to be an incredible end-time transfer of wealth to fund the end-time harvest of souls, and God is getting ready to put His people into places of dominion, power, influence, and great wealth for this precise purpose. I know that this sounds like a tough job, but someone's got to do it! Do I hear any takers?

There are no limits and no boundaries! Those who prove their faithfulness in little, the Lord will entrust with a lot! (See Matthew 25:21, 23.)

Prayer and Promise Principles

- The Lord has given you and me—His children—special privilege and access to His supernatural, limitless supply.

- Money is a positive thing—it's an amplifier of blessings! And in the hands of good, godly people, money becomes a means to build God's kingdom and bless His people on earth.

- God isn't asking us to take a vow of *poverty*, but He is asking us to take a vow of *priorities*.

- God not only sees and cares about the enormous financial burdens that we live under, but He also has a specific plan to free us from those burdens!

- Prosperity, wealth, dominion, and influence were part of God's plan for mankind from the very beginning!

- When we truly put God first and do our best to obey His Word, He will honor His promises and bless everything we put our hands to.

- Giving to God is a choice that we make by faith as we trust His promise to provide for our needs.

- God isn't after our money; He's after our hearts.

Chapter Sixteen

GOD'S SUPERNATURAL SUPPLY

God is providing for us a path to connect His supernatural supply to our daily needs. Let's get back to the Lord's Prayer. In the last chapter, we discussed the part that says, *"Thy kingdom come. Thy will be done in earth, as it is in heaven"* (Matthew 6:10). Is there any lack, debt, or poverty in heaven? Of course not! Lore has it that the streets are paved with gold! So when we pray, *"Thy kingdom come…in earth, as it is in heaven,"* we're technically praying for financial prosperity! If there is no poverty in heaven, then let's not accept poverty in our lives here on earth! If there is no lack or insufficiency in heaven, then let's put our feet down, rebuke it, and cast it out of our lives! Nothing but the will of God!

In Matthew 6:11, Jesus further instructed His disciples to ask the Father, *"Give us this day our daily bread."* I think that most Bible scholars would agree that this is referring to our daily needs in the physical realm, not in the spiritual or emotional realm. In this life, we have many spiritual and emotional needs, and our God has a plan to meet every one of them. But He also understands how many financial needs we have on a day-to-day basis. He is specifically inviting us to ask for His daily help, assistance, equipping, and blessings! He is providing for us a path to connect His supernatural supply to our daily needs! He is allowing us to break free from the limitations and shortages of this natural world and to tap into His miraculous, unlimited, supernatural help and resources! What an amazing and wonderful God we serve!

You know, Larry and I face the same giants that you do. We have a big vision, which requires big resources! We have the *vision*, but we still need the *provision!* We've been living on the edge and always pressing to new levels for more than thirty years, trusting God to bring in the provision to complete His vision.

Over the years, the Lord has shown and proven to us that where He guides, He also provides! He doesn't intend for us to figure out—nor will He necessarily show us—the entire financial projection for the upcoming future. Sometimes, the more we analyze our budgets and anticipate what the financial future will bring, the more anxious we become! Looking too far down the road of life and counting up the large amounts of money and resources that will be required is likely to overwhelm us.

By no means am I saying that we should neglect long-term planning or be careless with our spending. But there is a peace that comes to us when we realize that the Lord has a plan for our future provision—and it starts with today's provision!

That is exactly why we're to take it one day at a time. We are to pray, *"Give us **this day** our daily bread"* (emphasis added). We just need to focus on the provision that we need for today! We don't need to fret and worry about every need that lies ahead. As Jesus said, *"Do not worry about tomorrow, for tomorrow will worry about itself. Each day has enough trouble of its own"* (Matthew 6:34 NIV).

> THE LORD KNOWS HOW MUCH WE CAN HANDLE AT ONE TIME. THAT'S WHY HE TOLD US TO PRAY FOR PROVISION FOR TODAY ALONE.

The Lord knows how much we can handle at one time. That's why He told us to pray for provision for today alone.

I believe that we all are going to get to the place where we have so much money that we'll struggle to figure out what to do with it all! Rather than budgeting our living, we'll be budgeting our giving! At this point, however, most of us are still in need of our daily finances to pay for our daily bread—our grocery bills, mortgages, and car payments!

So, when you pray, tell the Lord what your current needs are and believe Him to release His miraculous provision. When God sent manna to feed the Israelites as they were traveling through the wilderness, He didn't send a year's provision for them to store up and ration out. No, each morning, when they woke up hungry, there was enough manna to fill their bellies for that particular day!

As we move forward in God's will, His plans, provisions, and equipping unfold before our very eyes. This is how we stay connected to God's supernatural supply and divine help. We can stay healthy and retain our sanity by remaining dependent on Him and not just relying on our own abilities, strengths, or cleverness. For me, it's very comforting to know that I don't have to figure everything out on my own. God has the big picture all laid out, and all we have to do is reach out through prayer and connect His super to our natural. What a reassuring truth!

What the Devil Steals, God Restores

As we discussed in the previous chapter, the Bible tells us that God has given us power over all the works of the enemy. One of the enemy's favorite ways to bring turmoil and stress into our lives is through our finances. Ecclesiastes 10:19 says, *"Money is the answer for everything"* (NIV). The entire world revolves around commerce. No matter how spiritual we are, we all have to pay our bills.

When we reach the end of our money before we reach the end of the month, our peace and tranquility experience more than just a little havoc! Nothing makes the enemy happier than to see God's people consumed by financial anxieties and struggles. I really don't even like to talk about the enemy or give him any credit or glory, but the Word tells us in Ephesians 6:11 to *"stand against the wiles of the devil."* Another word for *"wiles"* is strategies. Let's make sure we realize that the enemy has a strategy to rob, steal, and devour our finances every day! His goal is to wear us down and deplete our resources. The devil will try to distract us from our spiritual lives with a bombardment of financial burdens, from fines to debt to interest. But 2 Corinthians 2:11 says *"that Satan might not outwit us. For we are not unaware of his schemes"* (NIV). If we understand the schemes of Satan, he will not succeed in outwitting us.

Exercising Authority

God has given us power over all of the works of the devil, but it's up to us to exercise that authority. *It isn't automatic!* Through the power of the blood of Jesus, we can cancel the plans of the enemy, rebuke the spirit of the devourer, break every generational curse of poverty and failure, and crush the spirit of containment over our finances! You and I work too hard in life to let the enemy steal one single penny from us. The only power that he can have over us is the power that we allow him to take. When the devil sends you an evil report, reject it in prayer and send it right back to him in an envelope stamped RETURN TO SENDER. Again, remember our assurance from Isaiah 54:17: *"No weapon that is formed against thee shall prosper; and every tongue that shall rise against thee in judgment thou shalt condemn."*

> THROUGH THE POWER OF THE BLOOD OF JESUS, WE CAN CANCEL THE PLANS OF THE ENEMY, REBUKE THE SPIRIT OF THE DEVOURER, BREAK EVERY GENERATIONAL CURSE OF POVERTY AND FAILURE, AND CRUSH THE SPIRIT OF CONTAINMENT OVER OUR FINANCES!

Breaking the Spirit of Containment over Our Finances

The spirit of containment can work in our finances at any level. We may be struggling to make ends meet and just not be able to get ahead, or we may have achieved a comfortable financial level where we're fairly secure. At either end of the spectrum, the spirit of containment can be at work to keep us from progressing to the next financial level.

Even when we arrive at more comfortable financial levels, the Lord has higher levels that He wants to take us to. He always wants to bless us more and more so that we can be greater blessings to more and more people. When we desire all that the Lord has for us, we will never plateau in any area of our lives. His mercies and blessings are fresh every day. Each morning, let's expect our God to amaze us!

Jesus said to pray, *"Give us this day our daily bread"* (Matthew 6:11). This indicates that every day, the Lord has provision for us, but we still have to pray it into our lives. Each day presents new needs in our lives, and so each day, we need God's specific provision for those specific needs. The Bible tells us that God knows what we need before we even ask (see Matthew 6:8)—but we still have to ask.

Wealth Is a Blessing; Poverty and Debt Are Burdens

Out of all the needs that people ask us to pray for, probably the most frequent requests are for financial miracles. We all live in a real world with real financial obligations. It's a fact of life. Again, the Bible even tells us, *"Money is the answer for everything"* (Ecclesiastes 10:19 NIV). We see miracles all the time as we pray for God's provision and financial blessings in people's lives. Let me share a few testimonies to further confirm the reality of God's provision.

Evelyn Gets Her Dream Job

At one of our Miracle Services, a woman came for prayer and asked us to agree with her that the Lord would get her a good job. She was employed, but she desired to work someplace else that had a pleasant atmosphere, as well as offered her more opportunities to advance and earn a higher salary.

The following Sunday, she reported her miracle to us, saying, "Thank you for praying with me! Not only did the Lord answer my prayer, but He did it within six days! He opened a door for a really good job with great benefits, many opportunities to advance, and a lot more pay! He really is a great and mighty God!"

Disaster Launches Tammy into the Blessings of God

One of my favorite stories of blessing is from my friend Tammy. Tammy and her children were living in New Orleans when Hurricane Katrina hit. I asked her to write out her testimony for me to share, and she agreed. Here it is in her own words.

"My teenage kids and I came to Texas after losing everything in Hurricane Katrina. We were devastated by this disaster. We had nothing left. We were placed in government-provided emergency housing. It was very scary for us all. We had seen Pastor Huch and Tiz on TV and knew they were in Dallas. We found a way to get to their church on a Sunday morning. Pastor Tiz came up to me and introduced herself. When I told her of our current situation, she prayed with me. The very next week, I got a job making $10,000 more than I was making in New Orleans! My kids all got great jobs over the next few weeks, too! We have each received multiple raises, promotions, and supernatural favor!

"Over the last two years at New Beginnings, we have learned how to take the Word and apply it to our lives. The blessings of God have been poured onto our lives. We have bought and paid off a nearly new SUV, and we just closed on our brand-new home! I believe that through Pastor Larry and Tiz's teachings on faith and wise financial management, my home will be paid off soon, also!

"The greatest blessing of all, though, is that my four kids and I are all members of DFW New Beginnings and serving God together! As for me and my house, we will serve the Lord!"

Maria and Louis Receive Promotions

At one of our special Miracle Services a few months ago, Larry told the members of our congregation to take the limits off of their faith. "What do you want?" he asked, then challenged them to imagine their biggest dreams and ask God for them.

The next week, we received a praise report from Maria and Louis, a couple in our church. Maria wrote, "When Pastor asked us, 'What do you want?' I knew it was a word for me and my family! Our expectation exploded as we grabbed hold of God's promises! We have been serving in the church as ushers and are faithful givers. Our desire is for higher-paying jobs so that we can give more and enjoy the blessings of God with our family.

"The morning after the Miracle Service, I received a call from my boss offering me the position of Divisional Manager. He said I would be making over $100,000 a year! Added to that, he offered my husband a promotion, increasing his salary by $5000 a year! All in all, our household income literally tripled overnight! We are also getting company cars with paid insurance. Thank you, Pastors Larry and Tiz, for bringing us the Word of faith and expectation! Glory to God!"

Adrian's Dreams Come True

A woman named Adrian wrote us and told us her amazing story. She had gone through some tough times, both emotional and financial, for several long years. Then she walked into our church, New Beginnings. She wrote, "After studying and following the teachings of Pastors Larry and Tiz, something began to change in me, and my dreams grew bigger. I saw myself as the head of a large real-estate company rather than my small company. I felt a vision stir within me, and I began to make plans and prepare for growth. As I prayed about my company, the Lord gave me a clear vision of what I needed to do to take it to the next level. I was a little nervous about being able to handle the level of growth that I felt I was about to enter into, but I knew God would connect all the dots. I wanted to build a great and prosperous company that would be able to sow large amounts of money into God's kingdom.

"At the next church service, I sowed a large financial seed toward my dream. The next week, I received a call from a counterpart of mine about a house I had listed. As we chatted, I shared my vision and dream for my company with him. Amazingly, he had a similar vision for his own company. We ended up making plans to join our two companies together.

"Since we have implemented this merger, my business has doubled and is growing in leaps and bounds every week! I have been able to give more money to the Lord this month than I did for all of last year! Our God really does make dreams come true! Thank you for teaching me to trust God!"

Cheryl Gets a Better Job

A woman named Cheryl came to me after a service and told me that she had been laid off from her job. She asked me to agree with her for a better job that would earn more money. She wasn't complaining or moping;

she was full of faith and expectancy. We prayed and agreed together in faith. The next Sunday, she ran to me with a huge smile on her face and told me that the Lord had done exactly what we had asked Him to do! He had given her a great new job that earned more money!

Fred Receives Miraculous Provision

A man named Fred from Minnesota wrote to us and said, "Thank you for your ministry. I never miss your TV program. I have a drywall business that had done really well until the current economic downturn. The construction business has been really slow, and I have been having a tough time making ends meet. One day, while watching your program, I made the decision to start speaking faith promises over my business and sow a seed toward my financial breakthrough. Since I started giving to your ministry, I have received more work and many more financial miracles, which seem to pop up out of the blue! I love it! The more I give, the more God gives me. The more He gives me, the more I give back! God is so good! God bless you! Keep up the good work!"

A New Beginning and Financial Blessings

For years, Diane and Gerald had been watching our TV program. When the economy took a downturn in their state, they decided to step out in faith and move to Dallas to become a part of our church. They asked the Lord to give them a new beginning. The Lord has certainly done that—and more! They reported to us that they had secured wonderful dream jobs, were buying their own home, and were enjoying life for the first time in many years. Not only are they being financially blessed, but also, their children are coming back to the Lord, and God is restoring everything that the enemy had stolen from them. That's what I call a new beginning!

Gail Breaks the Spirit of the Devourer over Her Finances

After hearing a message about speaking God's promises in faith, a woman named Gail came for prayer. She said that her ex-husband had not paid any alimony or child support for years, and she was struggling as her family's sole financial supporter. During the service, something had brought her to the realization that the time had come for her to have a financial breakthrough. She decided that she wasn't going to let the devourer rob and steal from her any longer. A righteous anger rose up in her spirit—not against her husband, but against the enemy—the thief who comes to steal, kill, and destroy. (See John 10:10.)

> SHE HAD CALLED UPON GOD TO HELP HER, TO BLESS HER, AND TO PROVIDE WHAT WAS RIGHTFULLY HERS. AND BECAUSE SHE TOOK OWNERSHIP OF THE WORD, HER MIRACLE WAS RELEASED!

As Gail and I prayed together, we bound the spirit of lack and devouring and released the blessings of God into her finances. We called in every dollar that was meant to be in her hands and in her bank account. She refused to accept the enemy's report of insufficiency and chose to believe instead God's promise to supply increase and abundance.

By the time Gail came back to church on Wednesday night, several months' worth of child support funds had appeared in her bank account with no explanation! She had never called her ex-husband to demand any back payments. She had called upon God to help her, to bless her, and to provide what was rightfully hers. And because she took ownership of the Word, her miracle was released!

Alicia Prays in God's Supernatural Provision

A young lady named Alicia who watches us on TV wrote to us to thank us for imparting to her a fire and a faith to seek after all that the Lord has for her. She explained how God had blessed her in that she had been chosen to represent the United States in the World Championship of Performing Arts. This was a great honor that also presented a great challenge, for Alicia would be responsible for raising funds in order to cover the cost of participating in this event.

Alicia had no close family or friends to turn to for financial support. While watching our TV program, she was inspired to trust the Lord to provide the necessary funds, and she prayed and asked Him to help her. Mere minutes after her prayer, the phone rang. The caller was a prominent local business owner who said that although they had never met, he had heard about Alicia's opportunity and was impressed by her accomplishments. He went on to say that he knew participating in the event would be costly and that he wanted to host a major fund-raising drive for her!

Alicia hung up the phone and was jumping and shouting for joy when the phone rang again. It was a distant aunt who hadn't spoken with Alicia in years but had suddenly felt impressed to call her niece to see if she needed any money. After Alicia had described her exciting opportunity, her aunt told her, "Now I know why the Lord had me call you! I'll pay for half of your expenses."

In her letter to us, Alicia wrote, "Thank you for encouraging me to press in to my dreams and to never limit God. Praise God—He is a Father to the fatherless! Thank you for your prayers. They are powerful and effective, even reaching into another state!"

From Welfare to Owning Two Homes

A couple in our church gave us a praise report of how the Lord has blessed them through the years. Joanne told us that she had gotten pregnant as a sixteen-year-old and had lived off welfare for ten years as a single mother. She disliked being financially dependent upon the government, but she had no alternative. At the age of twenty-six, Joanne met Tom. They got married and decided to start attending church for the sake of the child. They came to New Beginnings, where they ended up giving their lives to the Lord. Their conversion was dynamic, and it set them on an entirely new course for their futures. They jumped into our ministries and activities with fervor and enthusiasm.

> GOD BEGAN TO BLESS THEM WITH RAISES, PROMOTIONS, AND ALL KINDS OF FAVOR, AND THEIR GIVING INCREASED CONTINUALLY AS THE LORD CONTINUED TO BLESS THEM.

As Joanne and Tom heard our teachings on faith and prosperity, they took personal ownership of the promises of God. They immediately began tithing and giving as generously as their incomes would allow. God began to bless them with raises, promotions, and all kinds of favor, and their giving increased continually as the Lord continued to bless them. Over the years, their family has grown, and they have increased their leadership roles in our church.

In their recent praise report, Joanne said, "We want to thank you for teaching us how to trust God and to put faith-demands on His promises. Through your teachings and example, Tom and I are the proud new owners of two homes! We live in one and rent the other one. You have taught us about biblical finances and sowing and reaping. You have also taught us success principles about the business world. You have motivated us and encouraged us to go beyond the natural realm and press into the supernatural realm of God's prosperity. You have blazed a clear trail that we have followed. We are being blessed beyond our wildest dreams, and we have been able to *be* a blessing beyond anything we ever could have imagined. We have so much more to do!"

An Anointing on the Word to Create

The Word of God is like a seed, and it has a powerful anointing to create. In 1 Corinthians 15:37–38, Paul explained, *"When you sow, you do not plant the body that will be, but just a seed, perhaps of wheat or of something else. But God gives it a body as he has determined, and to each kind of seed he gives its own body"* (NIV). God has put something miraculous within the seed of His Word that gives it the ability to reproduce itself. Isn't that amazing? When we pray and speak out the promises of God from His Word, He breathes life into them and causes them to come alive in us. The Lord has promised us, *"My word…that goeth forth out of my mouth…shall not return unto me void, but it shall accomplish that which I please, and it shall prosper in the thing whereto I sent it"* (Isaiah 55:11).

That is why it's critical that we saturate our minds with the Word. We've got to learn what God has promised us in His Word about our finances, take ownership of those promises, and then pray, speak them out, and work the Word until we possess those promises of God!

Let's get serious about learning, absorbing, and appropriating the Word and the promises of God. His will for our lives is not for us to continue struggling financially and barely getting by. As Larry says, "His name is not El-Get-By—His name is El Shaddai!" He is the God of more than enough, and His will is for His children to be greatly blessed so that they can be great blessings to others. We've got to stop letting the enemy bully and intimidate us! Put your foot down and declare the covenant blessings of God over your finances and your future!

Through prayer, let's put the enemy in his rightful place—under our feet and under our dominion and authority! Then, let's put God in His rightful place—exalted on high, almighty, all-powerful, the Creator and Ruler of all things! Let's pray some blessings and provisions into our lives.

Let's Pray!

Father God, we come to You in the name and the power of Jesus. We thank You for the privilege of knowing You and having access to all of Your blessings. We come boldly to the throne of grace to obtain help in our times of need. Thank You for Your divine favor, grace, and mercy. Thank You for Your supernatural equipping, provision, and supply. We know that Jesus came so that we could have life—and life more abundantly.

Forgive us, Lord, for any sins or wrongdoing in our hearts, our minds, and our bodies. Cleanse us and make us new. Forgive us for any doubts or fears that would keep us from trusting You. We exchange our doubts for Your faith, our fears for Your confidence, our weakness for Your strength, and our limitations for Your limitless supply.

Lord, You are Jehovah Jireh. We pray as You have instructed us to: give us this day our daily bread, needs, supplies, and provision. Thank You that it is Your will to bless us by enduing us with the power to prosper and excel. You have promised to give us Your favor—Your assistance, support, and privilege. We walk in Your divine favor! We thank You for Your divine grace—Your supernatural equipping—to do what we can't do by ourselves. We're not begging You for these things; we are simply acknowledging who You are and claiming what You have already done.

You are a merciful God, always willing to help us. We don't come to You as unworthy beggars. We come as Your children, joint-heirs with Jesus Christ. We love You, Lord, and we know that You love us, so we enter into the fullness of all that You have for us.

We step into Your anointing and Your equipping. Anoint us. Endue us with Your abilities to do all that You've called us to do. We tap into Your supernatural wisdom, gifts, and creativity. Let Your Spirit rise up on the inside of us, enabling us to fulfill the destinies that You have planned for us. And as we pursue these destinies, Father, go before us, with us, and after us, confirming Your Word with signs, wonders, and miracles.

Father, Your Word reminds us to say,

Bless the LORD, *O my soul, and forget not all his benefits: who forgiveth all thine iniquities; who healeth all thy diseases; who redeemeth thy life from destruction; who crowneth thee with lovingkindness and tender mercies.* (Psalm 103:2–4)

We thank You for the assurance in Romans 8:32: *"He that spared not his own Son, but delivered him up for us all, how shall he not with him also freely give us all things?"* Lord, we thank You for Your amazing love and for Your willingness to help us in every area of our lives.

Your very name is Jehovah Jireh, our Provider. We claim what Your Word says in Psalm 1:3: we *"shall be like a tree planted by the rivers of water, that bringeth forth his fruit in his season; his leaf also shall not wither; and whatsoever he doeth shall prosper."*

Father, we ask You to breathe Your breath of life into everything we put our hands to. Every place where we put the soles of our feet, You are giving us dominion. We claim Your promises from Deuteronomy to love us, bless us, and multiply the fruit in our families, our businesses, and everything we do. We're not out there on our own, Lord, but we are partnering with You in all of our endeavors.

You have promised us that You are the Lord our God who teaches us to profit (see Isaiah 48:17), who leads us in the way that we should go, and that we are like trees along a riverbank that bear much fruit every season. In Psalm 34:9, You have promised that *"there is no want [*"lack" NIV*] to them that fear"* You. We revere You, Lord, and trust that we will lack for nothing. Thank You, Lord, for the promise in Proverbs 22:4 that *"humility and the fear of the* LORD *bring wealth and honor and life"* (NIV).

Ecclesiastes 2:24–25 says, *"A man can do nothing better than to eat and drink and find satisfaction in his work. This too, I see, is from the hand of God, for without him, who can eat or find enjoyment?"* (NIV). It goes on to say, *"To the man who pleases him, God gives wisdom, knowledge and happiness"* (verse 26 NIV). Thank You for the privilege of taking pleasure in our work and earning wealth to advance Your kingdom. Wealth, possessions, and power that we earn through godly means are gifts from You for us to enjoy, as well as to use to bless others.

Father, You have said to us in Isaiah 1:19, *"If ye be willing and obedient, ye shall eat the good of the land."* Father, we accept, we claim, and we thank You for these promises right now!

In Malachi 3:10, You have commanded us, *"Bring the whole tithe into the storehouse, that there may be food in my house. Test me in this…and see if I will not throw open the floodgates of heaven and pour out so much blessing that you will not have room enough for it"* (NIV).

Father, You have challenged us to put You to the test and prove Your faithfulness to provide for our needs. So, as we are faithful in our giving to You, we know that You will be faithful to multiply our resources back to us.

Lord, we stand on Luke 6:38: *"Give, and it shall be given unto you; good measure, pressed down, and shaken together, and running over, shall men give into your bosom. For with the same measure that ye mete withal it shall be measured to you again."*

We claim Philippians 4:19: *"My God shall supply all your need according to his riches in glory by Christ Jesus."* Thank You, Lord, that You have promised us in 3 John 1:2 that Your will for each of us is *"that thou mayest prosper and be in health, even as thy soul prospereth."*

Father, I thank You for 2 Corinthians 9:8: *"God is able to make all grace abound toward you; that ye, always having all sufficiency in all things, may abound to every good work."* Father, we know that You will bring to pass every dream that You put in our hearts and every vision that You give to us to accomplish so that we will be able to fulfill the callings You have placed upon our lives.

We thank You for Proverbs 10:22, which tells us, *"The blessing of the LORD, it maketh rich, and he addeth no sorrow with it."* We ask You to apply Your super to our natural and to anoint us in our finances, careers, businesses, and ministries. Endue us with Your abilities. Equip us to do exceedingly, abundantly above all that we could ask or think!

Give us knowledge and discretion; give us wisdom, insight, and prudence. Give us unprecedented favor in our jobs, in our affairs, and in everything that we put our hands to. Cause our employers to have favor on us—their employees—and open doors of opportunity to us.

Now, Lord, we put our foot down and claim nothing but the will of God over our finances! We bind every spirit of the devourer on our lives. We rebuke every plan of the enemy for our finances and our futures. We command the spirit of containment to be broken over our finances. We break the spirit and the burden of debt over our lives and our families. We shred every curse of poverty, lack, and insufficiency. We break and shatter the glass ceilings over our jobs, businesses, and ministries. We rebuke every spirit of the enemy and every curse that would try to block Your financial blessings from our lives, our families, our children, our businesses, and our churches—once and for all!

We thank You, Lord, that every curse is broken and reversed, and that every blessing is being released in us, for us, and through us! We ask You to breathe Your breath of life into every seed that we have ever sown and to multiply it back a hundredfold in this lifetime. We call every unharvested seed into our pockets, our checkbooks, and our bank accounts. We claim every dollar that You have intended to be in our hands, and we call it in through the blood of Jesus.

We call in abundance, overflow, and increase. We call in raises, inheritances, back pay, child support and alimony. We even call in the wealth that was meant to be in the hands of the past generations. We claim the finances that have been held up, and we release them in Jesus' name! We release the spirit of prosperity into our lives.

We take the limits and boundaries off of our thinking, off of our lives, and off of our futures. We tap into Your unlimited flow of ideas, creativity, and resources. We declare, "No limits and no boundaries!" We know that Your very names are Jehovah Jireh—our Provider, and El Shaddai—the God of more than enough. We count it all done in the powerful and almighty name of Jesus Christ! Thank You, Lord, for Your incredible outpouring of blessings in us, for us, and through us!

Hallelujah! Let's shout some praise to seal this prayer. Amen—so be it in our lives!

PRAYER AND PROMISE PRINCIPLES

+ God specifically invites us to ask for His daily help, assistance, equipping, and blessings! He provides for us a path to connect His supernatural supply to our daily needs!
+ Where God guides, He also provides!
+ God has the big picture all laid out, and all we have to do is reach out through prayer and connect His super to our natural.
+ When the devil sends you an evil report, reject it in prayer and send it right back to him in an envelope marked RETURN TO SENDER.
+ God always wants to bless us more and more so that we can be greater blessings to more and more people.

- When we pray and speak out the promises of God from His Word, He breathes life into them and causes them to come alive in us.
- Put your foot down and declare the covenant blessings of God over your finances and your future!

Chapter Seventeen

FORGIVE US OUR DEBTS, AS WE FORGIVE OUR DEBTORS

At this point of our prayer based on the pattern Jesus gave us in the Lord's Prayer, we need to take a minute or two and do a little soul-searching. The truth is that this part of the prayer is a pivotal point in the process of receiving answers to our prayer requests. The ball is in our court, so to speak. The basis for salvation is receiving forgiveness from God for our sins, but if we expect God to forgive us of all our sins and wrongdoings, then we must first forgive others of their wrongdoings toward us. This part of the Lord's Prayer supports what Jesus said in Matthew 6:14–15: *"If ye forgive men their trespasses, your heavenly Father will also forgive you: but if ye forgive not men their trespasses, neither will your Father forgive your trespasses."*

How Do We Deal with Our Emotional Pain and Hurt?

We all know that forgiving is easier said than done. Forgiveness is one of the toughest issues that any of us faces, and yet the Lord commands us to forgive, even when our debtors don't deserve it. After all, God forgave us even though we didn't deserve it—*"While we were yet sinners, Christ died for us"* (Romans 5:8).

If the Lord expects us to live in an attitude of forgiveness, then He must make available the equipping to enable us to do so. Every one of us has wrestled with the emotional hurt and pain that result from an unjust act, mean-spirited words, or another form of injury. How do we find the strength to forgive in the midst of the emotional turmoil consuming our minds and hearts? In our lives, we are continually vulnerable to words and actions that threaten to hurt us, embarrass us, or put us down. What do we do with all of the wounds that result from these episodes?

Remember the childhood chant, "Sticks and stones may break my bones, but words will never hurt me"? Every child quickly figures out that there isn't even the smallest shred of truth in that saying. In fact, our wounded bodies often heal much more rapidly than our wounded hearts.

Over the course of my life, I have learned a lot about forgiveness, and I have counseled and prayed with many people through terrible, tragic events and injustices. It often seems impossible to endure the pain caused by another person, but our God always makes a way.

Live by Romans 8:28

> NO MATTER HOW DEEPLY WE HAVE BEEN HURT, GOD CAN TURN THE SITUATION AROUND AND MAKE IT WORK OUT FOR OUR BENEFIT.

Larry and I live by Romans 8:28, which says, *"And we know that all things work together for good to them that love God."* This verse provides tremendous comfort when you can't see or even imagine how a difficult situation will work out. God always finds a way to take the enemy's attack and turn it into something good and beautiful. He takes the loose ends of our lives and weaves them into a beautiful, complex tapestry. Focusing on this promise is a great help when it comes to forgiving people for the sins they commit against us. No matter how deeply we have been hurt, God can turn the situation around and make it work out for our benefit. Larry and I have watched this Scripture play out in our lives for more than thirty years. This is not just a comforting quotation on a Hallmark card; this is a promise from God's mouth that we can base our lives upon! We must choose to live in the freedom of forgiveness.

Choose to Forgive

The first step to forgive another person is making the choice to do so. Forgiveness doesn't start with a feeling; it starts with a choice. It isn't something we're naturally inclined to do, especially when the emotional wounds someone has inflicted on us are particularly deep.

When I was born again, I was feisty, strong-willed, high-spirited, and highly opinionated. I was living with four other brand-new Christians who were also feisty, strong-willed, high-spirited, and highly opinionated young ladies! As young ladies do from time to time, we had some very heated arguments.

On one occasion, we had a heated argument over a major crisis—probably a disagreement about whose turn it was to clean the bathroom or some other equally monumental issue. Anyway, we all got pretty mean, nasty, and ugly, and we said some very hurtful things to one another. We reached a sort of stalemate with no way out. So, we took our issues to our pastor, who, of course, advised us to forgive, forget, and make up.

This was good, sound, spiritual advice—but there was only one problem. Each of us had wounded—and been wounded by—the others. We all knew that we needed to get over it, but significant emotional damage had been done, and we didn't know how to get past our hurt feelings. Sound familiar? Of course it does! We have all faced similar situations with the same results. We know in our minds what needs to be done, but our hearts won't line up. As Jesus said in Matthew 26:41, *"The spirit indeed is willing, but the flesh is weak."*

Fake It Till You Make It

Sensing our pessimism about forgiving and forgetting, our wise pastor gave us a simple little illustration that I have repeated hundreds of times over the years to myself and to many others. He said that if you are going to try to build a solid concrete wall, you can't just pour concrete and expect it to stand up on its own and form a wall. You first have to build a temporary wooden structure and then pour the wet concrete into it. The temporary wooden structure is never meant to be the permanent solid wall, but it is a necessary transition piece. When the concrete finally hardens and becomes

> SOMETIMES, IT IS NECESSARY FOR US TO "PUT ON" FORGIVENESS AND CREATE A TEMPORARY STRUCTURE THAT WILL ENABLE US TO FORGIVE AND MOVE ON.

solid, we can tear down the temporary wooden structure, and we have our permanent wall. In other words, fake it till you make it!

The permanent concrete wall that we are trying to create is a forgiving heart free of bitterness and resentment. The way that we build it is by first putting up the temporary structure—choosing to forgive and then acting like we have forgiven the person. Sometimes, it is necessary for us to "put on" forgiveness and create a temporary structure that will enable us to forgive and move on.

Once we have built the temporary structure of forgiveness, God can pour the real thing—and the sense of freedom and release that results—into our hearts. This is how we achieve a permanent structure of clean, pure, forgiving hearts.

Choose to Live in Forgiveness Daily

Every day, we must make the decision to live in forgiveness. This forgiveness is not only for the sins that others commit against us that day, but also for past events that our minds rehearse and rehash.

One day, I was driving and wasn't really thinking about anything in particular (including my driving), when I suddenly realized that for the past ten minutes, I had been replaying a situation in my head that had happened more than two years prior. Out of nowhere, the memory of what an individual did to us popped into my head, and I held it there. In my mind, I was reliving the whole scenario, rehearsing what I should have done or said and considering what I still could say to get even with that person. This went on without my notice for a while, and the next thing I knew, I was driving 55 mph in a 25-mph zone! My shoulders were tensed, my hands were holding the steering wheel with a death grip, my heart was racing, and I was even angrier than I had been two years earlier when the situation occurred.

Suddenly, I came to my senses, slammed on the brakes, loosened my grip, shook my shoulders, and snapped myself out of it. I said aloud to myself, "Hey! Get over it! That situation is long gone. I did what I could at the time; it is what it is, but it is over. Now, get over it!"

I had chosen to forgive that person two years previously, and I choose to forgive him now. I'm not going to give one more ounce of energy to reliving that scene! I've already given it all to the Lord, so it's in His hands, not mine. Have you ever heard the Lord say to you, "Do you want to handle this on your own, or do you want Me to handle it?" Well, I have, and He can certainly do a better clean-up job than we can do ourselves.

Someone may have harmed your past, but don't let him harm your future, too! I've decided that I am more interested in my future than I am in my past. I am more concerned about creating a wonderful future than I am about dwelling on a painful past. How about you?

Repentance Is a Gift

I want us to think differently about the reason the Lord tells us to repent and forgive. To repent of something basically means to stop committing that action and to turn around and go in the opposite direction. God does not expect us to be perfect, but He does expect us to make deliberate attempts to move forward and leave our sinful behaviors behind rather than moving backward or standing still. As the analogy goes, the church is like a body and fender repair shop, with various wrecks in various stages of repair. We aren't perfect, but through Christ, we're being perfected.

Always keep in mind that the Lord's commands that keep us on course are not so much for *His* sake as they are for *our own* sakes. He loves us so much that He wants the absolute best for us, but sometimes, we act in ways that keep the absolute best from reaching us. The things that God tells us to steer clear of are usually the things that could end up hurting or even destroying us.

> ALWAYS KEEP IN MIND THAT THE LORD'S COMMANDS THAT KEEP US ON COURSE ARE NOT SO MUCH FOR HIS SAKE AS THEY ARE FOR OUR OWN SAKES.

Repentance is a gift from God! It's like taking a shower for our souls. Statistics show that the root of most mental illness is unresolved guilt, bitterness, and hatred. Think about that. God knows the terrible toll of sinful behaviors and wrong choices on our minds, emotions, souls, and bodies. This is why He created another path for a divine exchange: repentance.

Beauty for Ashes

In Matthew 11:28, Jesus told us, "*Come unto me, all ye that labour and are heavy laden, and I will give you rest.*" In Luke 4:18–19, Jesus quoted the prophet Isaiah to explain the purpose of His anointing. He said,

> *The Spirit of the Lord is upon me, because he hath anointed me to preach the gospel to the poor; he hath sent me to heal the brokenhearted, to preach deliverance to the captives, and recovering of sight to the blind, to set at liberty them that are bruised, to preach the acceptable year of the Lord.*

The passage He quoted from Isaiah reads,

> *The spirit of the Lord GOD is upon me; because the LORD hath anointed me to preach good tidings unto the meek; he hath sent me to bind up the brokenhearted, to proclaim liberty to the captives, and the opening of the prison to them that are bound; to proclaim the acceptable year of the LORD, and the day of vengeance of our God; to comfort all that mourn; to appoint unto them that mourn in Zion, to give unto them beauty for ashes, the oil of joy for mourning, the garment of praise for the spirit of heaviness; that they might be called trees of righteousness, the planting of the LORD, that he might be glorified.* (Isaiah 61:1–3)

What a wonderful picture of what God desires to do in our lives! However deep the injuries the enemy or the world has inflicted on our hearts, our families, or our lives, our God has amazing plans for our futures! Not only does He have compassion on our sufferings, but He also has the power and anointing to break every heavy burden off of us, to restore everything that the enemy has stolen, and to rock our world with blessings!

God does not condemn us for the things that cause us grief and heaviness or break our hearts. Rather, He feels grief for the very same reasons;

He sympathizes with our sufferings and weaknesses. (See Hebrews 14–15.) He offers us comfort, healing, and the anointing to be set free from the grip of all hurtful things.

We have a loving, compassionate God who allowed His own Son to be willingly beaten, bruised, scorned, and slaughtered so that you and I would not have to live under the oppression and entrapments of the world. Remember, our Father is never pointing a finger of accusation at us; He is reaching out a hand to help us!

> OUR FATHER IS NEVER POINTING A FINGER OF ACCUSATION AT US; HE IS REACHING OUT A HAND TO HELP US!

Another Divine Exchange

When we choose to turn away from our sins, hate them, and repent of them, the divine exchange takes place. The Spirit of God supernaturally lifts those things out of our hearts and replaces them with love, compassion, and forgiveness. Another great trade! There is nothing as liberating and as wonderful as coming clean before God and feeling the Holy Spirit cleanse our hearts, minds, and bodies. This experience brings true deliverance from all destructive, negative feelings and tumultuous emotions. Repentance is one of the greatest gifts the Lord has given to His children.

Accepting this gift and making the choice to repent, or turn away from, sins and unforgiveness unleashes a powerful force. When we choose to let go of unforgiveness, hurt, bitterness, and resentment, God supernaturally severs the tie that the hurtful action has on us. When you are hurt or violated, the harmful action has a hold on you that ties your heart, mind, and body to that action. But if you allow Him, God will cut that tie and protect you from all of its potentially harmful long-term effects. This is something that we can't do ourselves in the natural. Only God, through the power of His Spirit, can supernaturally do this.

When I pray for people who struggle with unforgiveness, I see a literal, physical transformation. The deliverance they experience on the inside shows on the outside; they are changed from the inside out, and it often looks as though they've had face-lifts. What they actually had were faith-lifts, which are less expensive but have results that last!

Let's lose the sense of shame and condemnation we tend to feel when dealing with anger and bitterness. Let's lighten up and look at the challenge to forgive as an incredible opportunity for the Lord to help us, set us free, and lift us to a higher level of His blessing. Learning to walk in a spirit of forgiveness is one of the greatest gifts we can give ourselves. So, as you move forward, don't take on a spirit of heaviness; take on a spirit of anticipation and excitement! You're about to enter into a whole new level of unspeakable joy and matchless glory.

Forgive for Your Health—A Medical Defense of a Biblical Mandate

Thank God for every medical breakthrough that we hear about. Researchers are continually coming up with more effective medicines and methods to treat illnesses and diseases. But even with advanced treatments, we would rather avoid developing conditions and catching illnesses than treat them after the fact, right? Studies have shown a strong link between anxiety, depression, anger, and other stress-related emotional conditions and such physical ailments as stomach ulcers, heart disease, and cancer. It has been accepted for many years that these destructive emotions are often linked to heart attacks.

We often overlook the link between our emotions and our physical health. But it is true that a complex interconnection exists between our bodies and our minds. Again, medical research is discovering the strong link between the conditions of our minds and hearts and the physical conditions of our bodies.

I heard a doctor speak about his conviction that bitterness, anger, and resentment can be the root causes of most major illnesses. He explained how stress, anxiety, and negative emotions create acid in our systems, which makes for a toxic internal environment. We all know that worry and anxiety can cause excess acid to build up in our stomachs, which can lead to ulcers and other stomach disorders. Now, we are learning that those acids are released into the bloodstream and through the internal organs. This doctor went on to explain that cancer, heart disease, high blood pressure, arthritis, diabetes, and many other harmful or deadly diseases thrive in toxic, acidic bodies. He said that a continual bombardment of these factors in our bodies breaks down our immune systems and hinders their abilities to defend us against sickness and disease. He concluded by saying, "Stress is a killer!"

> YOUR DEBTOR
> MAY HAVE
> HARMED YOUR
> PAST; DON'T LET
> HIM HARM YOUR
> FUTURE, TOO!

The Lord is adamant about our need to forgive and let go of bitterness because He loves us and doesn't want anything to block the wonderful futures He has planned for us. As I said before, your debtor may have harmed your past; don't let him harm your future, too!

A Hypothetical Study of the Consequences of Unforgiveness

Harboring unforgiveness and bitterness in our hearts is poisonous to our souls. Let me give you an illustration that you won't forget. Refusing to forgive someone is like drinking a poison yourself and waiting for the other person to get sick! We don't forgive someone for his sake; we forgive him for our own sake! If unforgiveness is like poison, the person you refuse to forgive won't get sick, but you will. One of the reasons we hold on to unforgiveness is that we feel that by not forgiving the person who wronged us, we're somehow punishing or getting even with him. But the truth is that we aren't punishing him; we're only prolonging our own hurt.

Let's consider a hypothetical situation. Jim and Laura have been married for eight years and have two children. Suddenly, Jim acts eccentrically and has a wild fling with little Miss Suzie Q. He then decides to divorce Laura and marry Miss Suzie Q, leaving poor Laura with nothing but heartaches, two children, and a stack of bills.

Heartbroken and flat broke, Laura becomes consumed by grief and sorrow, which quickly turn into anger and bitterness. Her thinking is colored by vindictiveness, resentment, and hatred. She dreams of performing sadistic rituals by candlelight with a voodoo doll of her ex-husband. Laura can't get over these terrible feelings and believes that she can't move on with her future.

This type of situation is devastating. But what will be even more devastating are the months and years of future living that will be destroyed if Laura lets these negative, toxic emotions engulf her and define who she becomes.

Although this story is fictitious, it represents thousands of true stories. Let's look a little more closely at what happens to Jim and Laura in the aftermath. Laura becomes more and more consumed by bitterness and unforgiveness, which take a serious toll on her health. She can't focus her thoughts, and her career starts to slip away. She finds it hard to make ends meet, and it becomes more difficult for her to get up in the mornings. She loses all hope and motivation; the future looks bleak and gloomy, and she cannot imagine ever being happy again. The only thoughts that stir her up are the schemes she plans to get even with Jim and Miss Suzie Q. She hangs on to unforgiveness because it seems like a way of taking revenge or getting back at them. Laura can't seem to move on.

Negative Emotions Are Not Only Toxic; They're Also Contagious

Unforgiveness takes a toll not only on Laura, but on her children, as well. They, too, feel the pain and stress caused by their parents' ugly divorce. They are dealing with their own emotional issues, as well as with the fallout from their mother's bitterness and depression. Negative emotions are not only toxic; they're also *contagious!*

Meanwhile, guess what? Jim and Miss Suzie Q have moved on! They're not sitting around thinking about Laura. They're living life, probably basking in the sun on a beach somewhere and sipping margaritas. They couldn't care less about the sequence of disastrous effects they have caused in Laura's life. While Laura dreams of getting even, Jim and Miss Suzie Q are off living their dreams. Laura's fixation on bitter revenge is not hurting those who caused her grief; instead, it's hurting only herself and her children, keeping her bound and captive to Jim's painful act of betrayal.

Who Suffers the Most from Unforgiveness?

So, who suffers the most from unforgiveness? Is it the person who hurt us, who couldn't care less and has moved on? Or, is it us? If we don't let go of unforgiveness, we can't move on. We hurt and hinder only ourselves. It is impossible to move forward into a new future when we are fixated on our pasts. Just try to walk forward with your head turned around, looking backward. It's difficult, isn't it? You're going to either stumble into a wall and fall down or spin in circles, going nowhere.

> IF WE DON'T LET GO OF UNFORGIVENESS, WE CAN'T MOVE ON. WE HURT AND HINDER ONLY OURSELVES.

Let this be a wakeup call for all of us. Let's not wait until we have to treat the symptoms—let's treat the *causes* so that we never get the symptoms! Unforgiveness, bitterness, and resentment take too high a toll for us to mess around with them. It just isn't worth the cost! Let's heed the warning in Proverbs 4:23 to guard our hearts with all diligence, for out of them come the issues of life. Our lives and futures spring out of the attitudes and conditions of our hearts, so it's vital to keep our heart conditions optimal—positive, joyful, and quick to forgive.

Unforgiveness Blocks the Blessings of God

This is why the Lord is so adamant about our need to forgive and let go of bitterness. He loves us and doesn't want anything to block the wonderful futures He has planned for us. As I said before, your debtor may have harmed your past; don't let him harm your future, too!

Unforgiveness creates a huge roadblock to receiving the blessings of God. To grasp the gravity of this fact, picture driving down a road and encountering a rockslide that has completely blocked both lanes, making it impossible to pass. Your wonderful destination is just beyond the pile of rocks, but you can't reach it because of the insurmountable roadblock. In just the same way, unforgiveness and bitterness create a spiritual roadblock that will bar you from God's blessings.

Let's decide right now that we are going to close the doors of our minds to these destructive, toxic, poisonous emotions! This applies to every negative thing that has happened to us in our pasts, is happening to us currently, or may happen to us in the future, God forbid.

Forgiveness Is an Incredible Force

The doctor I mentioned earlier was speaking about the effects of stress from a medical standpoint, not a spiritual standpoint. After calling stress a killer, he went on to say, "Unforgiveness is toxic! True forgiveness is extremely self-cleansing and healing. It sets you free from that act or that person who harmed you. It cuts the tie, cleanses you, and sets you free to move forward." These were the words of a medical doctor! He added, "Forgiveness is an incredible force. It emotionally sets you free from the pain, the hurt, and the anger, and then sets you in a place of healing and wholeness. It positions you toward seeing and entering into a beautiful future!"

This doctor was thinking on the same track as our heavenly Father, who taught us the same thing in the Scriptures. Forgiving and repenting are like taking a spiritual shower! They cleanse our hearts, minds, and bodies from the damaging effects of sin and bitterness. I love what the doctor said because it sounds just like what God said.

Furthermore, as we have already discussed, our God is a God of total restoration. Anything the enemy destroys or steals from us, our Lord promises to make him pay back to us. So, when the enemy reminds us of our past losses, let's remind him of his future obligations! Whenever Larry and I face anything that seems to be a setback or a loss, we keep our thoughts, words, and actions focused on the promise that God will make it up to us in the days ahead! And guess what? He always has, and He always will!

> OUR GOD IS A GOD OF TOTAL RESTORATION. ANYTHING THE ENEMY DESTROYS OR STEALS FROM US. OUR LORD PROMISES TO MAKE HIM PAY BACK TO US.

Anything that looks to us like a *setback* looks to God like a *setup*—and He isn't fazed. There is one prerequisite that we must meet, though, before He'll turn our setbacks around. We cannot be consumed with unforgiveness, bitterness, resentment, or self-pity. We must become consumed instead with forgiveness, compassion, love, and joy! If we do this, God can turn our trials into triumphs.

The hypothetical scenario I created of Jim and Laura was certainly an extreme case. But every day, dozens of less extreme hurtful events work to create roots of bitterness in our hearts and minds. We can't afford to let this happen. In our relationships with our spouses, children, other family members, friends, neighbors, coworkers, and fellow churchgoers, there are many opportunities every day to dish out offenses, as well as to receive them.

Pluck Out the Spirit of Bitterness by the Roots

The book of Hebrews admonishes us, *"Make every effort to live in peace with all men and to be holy; without holiness no one will see the Lord. See to it that no one misses the grace of God and that no bitter root grows up to cause trouble and defile many"* (Hebrews 12:14–15 NIV). I have known many people who have been bound by a spirit of bitterness. They are easily offended and seem to be constantly angry, whether they've been provoked or not. It seems that they have to transfer their bitterness from victim to victim. They walk around mad at the whole world, and their anger spills over onto every person who crosses their paths. These individuals are like walking time bombs ready to explode at the slightest provocation.

There are also individuals whom Larry and I refer to as "offense collectors." These people "collect" offenses and store them up in their minds and hearts while plotting to get even at a later date or to vindicate their anger.

This is precisely what the author of the letter to the Hebrews was talking about. We have to pluck that *"bitter root"* out of the soil of our hearts and never allow it to sprout and grow there again. As I mentioned earlier, problems that are not dealt with don't go away. They just go underground, only to resurface again later.

I'm not talking about just covering up our anger or using behavior modification techniques. I'm talking about letting God pluck that spirit of unforgiveness out by the roots! Picture those pesky weeds that keep popping up in your lawn or garden. If you merely mow them down, they'll grow right back. To eliminate them for good, you need to pull them up by the roots. The same truth applies to the roots of bitterness that sprout in our hearts.

In Larry's teaching on generational curses, he likes to reference Isaiah 53:5 and expound upon the word *iniquities*. Isaiah 53:5 reads, *"But he was wounded for our transgressions, he was bruised for our iniquities: the chastisement of our peace was upon him; and with his stripes we are healed."* In *Free at Last*, he writes that *"iniquity* means 'a wicked act or sin,' but the Holy Spirit has shown me that *iniquity* can also be understood as any spirit that tries to break us down. It is a spiritual force on the inside that pressures us to bow or bend under its destructive nature."[7]

In other words, *iniquity* identifies not only sinful actions but also the driving forces behind those actions.

> WITH THE POWER OF JESUS CHRIST, AND BECAUSE OF HIS ATONING BLOOD, WE CAN AND WILL BREAK THE CURSES THAT CAUSE US TO ACT IN DESTRUCTIVE WAYS.

With the power of Jesus Christ, and because of His atoning blood, we can and will break the curses that cause us to act in destructive ways. We're going to quit treating the symptoms over and over again and pluck out the cause by the roots! Life is too short and too precious to be wasted by wallowing in sorrows. Let's get past our pasts and grab ahold of our futures!

Continually Choose to Forgive

As we have discussed, the first step to forgiveness is *choosing* to forgive. The next step is *continually choosing* to forgive. No one else can control our thoughts for us—not even God. He can help us to change and transform, but forgiveness ultimately begins and continues with our own choices. We've already discussed what Paul wrote in 2 Corinthians 10:3–5 about fighting and winning spiritual battles by *"casting down imaginations, and every high thing that exalteth itself against the knowledge of God, and bringing into captivity every thought to the obedience of Christ"* (verse 5).

Philippians 4:4–8 is a similar passage with power. Verse 4 reads, *"Rejoice in the Lord always. I will say it again: Rejoice!"* (NIV). I guess that Paul knew we needed to hear it twice! He went on to say,

---

[7] Huch, *Free at Last*, 170.

Let your gentleness be evident to all. The Lord is near. Do not be anxious about anything, but in everything, by prayer and petition, with thanksgiving, present your requests to God. And the peace of God, which transcends all understanding, will guard your hearts and your minds in Christ Jesus. Finally, brothers, whatever is true, whatever is noble, whatever is right, whatever is pure, whatever is lovely, whatever is admirable—if anything is excellent or praiseworthy—think about such things. Whatever you have learned or received or heard from me, or seen in me—put it into practice. And the God of peace will be with you. (verses 5–9 NIV)

I have tried to practice the guidelines in this Scripture for the entirety of my Christian life. And before that, I had tried to practice the secular, common-sense versions: "If you don't have anything nice to say, don't say anything at all!" "Accentuate the positive; eliminate the negative!" "Don't focus on the bad stuff; focus on the good stuff!"

Whether we consider this principle from the biblical perspective or the common-sense perspective, following it makes for happier and more blessed minds, spirits, and bodies. We have the ability to choose the kinds of thoughts and emotions we will allow to rule and reign within us. Choose—and keep on choosing—positive, life-producing, fruit-bearing, godly characteristics. Take the high road! Choose life!

Don't Get Bitter. Get Better!

In our thirty-plus years of ministry, Larry and I have weathered significant hurt, betrayal, and slander. I guess it kind of goes with our job description. Not everyone who comes into our lives or church stays. Not everyone who hears our messages agrees with them. And not everyone who meets us loves us (even if that's hard to comprehend!).

Nevertheless, we have adopted a habit of not focusing on these things. We choose to focus instead on the positives in our lives and on what God's promises say about our futures. We have also learned to trust that God will always vindicate us. We apply Isaiah 54:17 to ourselves: "*No weapon* [or slander] *that is formed* [or spoken] *against* [us] *shall prosper.*" Taking this approach isn't always easy, but it is always possible! Trusting God and focusing on His promises have kept us from becoming bitter, cynical, harsh, and spiteful. At the same time, they have caused us to become more optimistic, loving, kind, and tender. We have learned to choose not to get bitter but to get better! It's another wonderful divine exchange!

A professional football player who is a professing Christian once spoke at our church, and he said something that really hit home. He told us, "The greatest advice my football coach ever gave to me was that I needed to learn how to develop amnesia. The coach told me, 'Without a doubt, you will make some mistakes. As long as you are in the game, you're going to fall down, and you're going to fumble and drop the ball and feel like a failure at times. But I need you to be able to get back up, learn from your mistakes, and then forget about them. Develop amnesia and move forward.'"

This advice applies not only to the playing field, but to all of life, as well. If we blow it and fall down, let's get back up, learn from our mistakes, forget about them—develop amnesia—and move forward. If we mess up again (and we know that we will), we'll repeat the preceding procedure!

> IF WE BLOW IT AND FALL DOWN, LET'S GET BACK UP, LEARN FROM OUR MISTAKES, FORGET ABOUT THEM—DEVELOP AMNESIA—AND MOVE FORWARD.

Life is a journey, and every day, we are presented with opportunities to become better or worse. As for you and me, I know that we are going to decide to become more godly with each new day.

Are you ready to move from talking about prayer to actually praying? Okay! As you read through this next part, say it out loud as a prayer to the Lord.

Let's Pray!

Father, we come before You in the name of Jesus and in the tremendous, cleansing power of His blood. Lord, we ask You to forgive us for all of our sins and wrongdoing. Forgive us for any impure or ungodly thoughts. If we have offended anyone today, and if we were edgy or short or disrespectful of anyone, forgive us and cleanse us. Help us not to be hurtful, uncaring, or unforgiving.

Keep us from being self-centered and from thinking more highly of ourselves than we ought to. Transform our negative thoughts, doubts, and fears into positive faith, hope, and confidence. Renew our minds and mold us into Your image. Replace our hearts and minds with Your heart and mind.

Father, as You are merciful to forgive us, we make the choice to forgive others. Forgive us for holding bitterness against those who have hurt or wronged us. Father, we forgive them, and we release them to You. We choose not to hold unforgiveness, bitterness, and anger in our hearts. We choose to let them go and to move forward into all that You have for us. We are able to do this because of our love for and obedience to You, and because we want the best that You have for us. Help us not to be quick to offend or be offended; help us to be quick to forgive and forget.

Father, we choose to take the high road. Father, we choose to focus on Your promises. We choose to walk in peace and with positive thoughts, words, and actions.

Cleanse our hearts, Lord. Cleanse our hearts and make us new people. Replace our wounds with Your love, Your forgiveness, and Your wholeness. We ask You to supernaturally turn our negative situations around. We know and trust Your promise that all things will work together for our good, and that You are going to create something wonderful and beautiful from even the ugliest aspects of our lives. We entrust our futures to You, our loving, caring Father.

From this moment forward, Lord, we focus only on Your promises. The past is past. We choose to move past our pasts through the power of the Holy Spirit working within us.

Right now, Lord, we ask You to set us free from the ties and bondages to the pains and hurts that we have experienced. We rebuke every spirit or seed of bitterness, hatred, and resentment through the blood of our Savior and Deliverer. We accept and claim Your supernatural deliverance right now, in Jesus' name! And we close the doors of our minds, our spirits, and our bodies to all tormenting emotions forevermore! We choose not to get bitter. We choose to get better!

We break every generational curse and pattern of negative thinking, negative speaking, anger, bitterness, and hatred. We break every curse that has come upon us from abuse or hurt. Through the blood of Jesus Christ, we rebuke every spirit that has ever attacked our lives and abused us in any way. In Jesus' name, we rebuke every spirit that has tried to rip us off and devour our lives, our resources, and our joy. We rebuke the enemy, who has come to steal, kill, and destroy. We resist the enemy, and he has to flee, in Jesus' name. Father, we cancel every plan of the enemy. We shred every plan that he has made for our lives, our families, and our futures. We cast down and cast out the negative forces that try to influence and control our thinking.

In Jesus' name, we cancel every spirit of oppression, every spirit of depression, every spirit of mental illness, and every spirit of suicide. We plead the blood of Jesus over our minds, our thoughts, our emotions, our spirits, and our bodies. We claim that every curse is broken and reversed!

Now, Lord, we claim our freedom, liberty, and deliverance. We release every generational blessing upon our lives, our families, and our futures. We thank You in advance for the complete restoration of everything the enemy has stolen or will steal from us. In fact, we claim Your promise in Proverbs 6:30–31 of a sevenfold return of what has been stolen or held back from us.

We release all of the stored-up blessings that have been held back from our lives and from the generations before us. We claim Your promise in Jeremiah 29:11 that You have plans for our lives that are not for evil but for good. We release all of Your joy, Your love, and Your goodness. Father, we acknowledge You for who you are, and we receive what You have already done for us. You are Jehovah Shalom—our Peace. You are Jehovah Jireh—our Provider. You are Jehovah Rophe—our Healer. You are Jehovah Rohi—our Guide and our Leader. Father, You go before us with a banner. Lord, You are our Protector. You are Jehovah Shammah—everything we need, whenever we need it.

Father, we choose life! We choose joy! We choose happiness! We choose today to walk in Your light, Your love, and Your goodness, through the blood of Jesus Christ. We know that You are watching over Your Word to perform it in our lives. And we praise You! In Jesus' name, amen.

Hallelujah! Now give Him a shout of praise!

Praise God! It feels like we just had a spiritual shower, doesn't it? Isn't that a great feeling? I'm proud of you, and I know the Lord is, too!

Each and every day, choose life!

Prayer and Promise Principles

- God always finds a way to take the enemy's attack and turn it into something good and beautiful.

- Forgiveness doesn't start with a feeling; it starts with a choice.

- When it comes to forgiveness, fake it till you make it!

- Repentance is a gift from God! It's like taking a shower for our souls.

- When we choose to let go of unforgiveness, hurt, bitterness, and resentment, God supernaturally severs the tie that the hurtful action had on us.

- Anything the enemy destroys or steals from us, our Lord promises to make him pay back to us.

- Unforgiveness is like drinking poison yourself and waiting for the other person to get sick!

- Choosing to forgive someone is not so much for that person's sake as it is for our own sakes—and for the Lord's sake.

Chapter Eighteen

LEAD US NOT INTO TEMPTATION, BUT DELIVER US FROM EVIL

Throughout this book, I have referred to prayer as a divine exchange by which we exchange our weaknesses for His strengths, our lack for His abundance, our fears for His courage, our doubts for His faith, and our limitations for His never-ending supply. But I have also tried to convey that what happens in prayer needs to compute in real life. What happens in the spiritual realm needs to alter what happens in the natural realm.

This is especially important as we explore the next to the last portion of the Lord's Prayer, *"Lead us not into temptation, but deliver us from evil"* (Matthew 6:13).

As I have done in the preceding chapters, in addition to teaching you how to pray, I'm teaching you how to *live out* your prayers. Prayer is never meant to be about merely the action of the hour; it's meant to affect all the actions and events of our lives. So, as we discuss this part of the Lord's Prayer, I want to talk about backing up our prayers with lifestyle choices.

First of all, I think a better way of praying this concept might be, "Lead us away from temptation and deliver us out of evil situations." I say this because the Word tells us that our God does not tempt us. (See James 1:13.) That is the enemy's job!

God Is Not Trying to Take Joy Away from Us; He's Trying to Get True Joy to Us!

We live in a world in which we are continually bombarded with pressures and temptations to conform to the ungodly influences of society. We live in a real world with real issues. But the Bible tells us that although we live in this world, we are not to conform to this world. (See Romans 12:2.)

Have you ever wondered exactly what that means or struggled with trying to live that out? How far are we meant to go to separate ourselves from the world? Every denomination or camp seems to have its own interpretations of this. In fact, some well-meaning groups go as far as to forbid women from putting on makeup or wearing contemporary clothing or cutting their hair. The other extreme is to blend and integrate with the world to the extent that there is absolutely no visible difference between Christians' lifestyles and conversations and those of secular society. One extreme *chokes* the life out of us; the other extreme *extracts* the life out of us! In our years of ministry, I think that Larry and I have seen it all!

> GOD'S PLAN IS NOT TO DEPRIVE US OF FUN AND GOOD TIMES; IT IS TO PLACE US ON A SOLID FOUNDATION THAT WILL LEAD US INTO TRUE AND LASTING HAPPINESS, FULFILLMENT, AND PEACE.

The Lord came to bring us life—and that more abundantly! Keeping His commandments is not meant to take pleasure away from our lives; it's meant to bring true pleasure to our lives! His plan is not to deprive us of fun and good times; it is to place us on a solid foundation that will lead us into true and lasting happiness, fulfillment, and peace.

Our so-called liberated society has produced a lot more than liberation—divorce, addictions, teen pregnancies, and sexually transmitted diseases are prevalent, and many penitentiaries and youth correctional facilities are overcrowded. All too often, the things that we think will add fun and excitement to our lives end up bringing pain and dead ends. The very things the world says will bring us joy end up wreaking havoc and confusion in our hearts. The paths intended to lead us to the fulfillment of our dreams can end up leading us into our worst nightmares! Our God has a wonderful, amazing plan that will lead us away from these destructive paths and put us on paths that will lead us into the joy and blessings that He desires and has destined for us.

He Has Set Apart Each of Us for a Special Purpose

Jeremiah 1:5 says, *"Before I formed you in the womb I knew you, before you were born I set you apart"* (NIV). Do you realize that God knows us better than we know ourselves? After all, He created us! He has set apart each of us for a special purpose and a particular work! We need to realize that fully serving God is not just a bunch of do's and don'ts. It's a bunch of get-to's, opportunities, and privileges!

No matter how great of a life you or I could carve out for ourselves, it would be nothing compared to the incredible, blessed life that our God has destined for us! The Lord always has our best interests in mind. God is a giver, not a taker. In fact, for those who follow His path, He promises to do exceedingly, abundantly above all that they can ask or think. (See Ephesians 3:20.) Given that plan, we can't go wrong!

Larry and I are living testimonies of this promise. For more than thirty years, our lifestyle has been characterized by mutual commitment to each other based upon the guidelines in God's Word. Living in accordance with the Word has kept us on a path that is wonderful, vibrant, and ongoing. Our commitment to God's guidelines has taken us through the rocky times in our marriage, stabilized us in times of doubt and uncertainty, and empowered us to remain flexible to change for the better. As a result, we have been led into our own personal Promised Land in our marriage, family, ministry, business, finances, and every other area of life!

By the grace of God, we have managed to create a strong, great, and happy marriage and to raise our children to become godly, well-adjusted, productive adults. We have proven that it's possible to live lives that are pure, holy, and moral, and yet still be modern and contemporary, fitting into today's society and living life to the max! To live a life *"set...apart"* doesn't mean that we have to act and dress strangely. Our goal as Christians is not to alienate the world. It is rather to draw the world to the goodness of God. We can be "normal" and contemporary while living clean, godly lives that reflect God's glory.

Life is always a balancing act, but there are absolutes from God's Word that we can use to build our lives upon. In the teachings on our CD called *Family Matters*, Larry and I have laid out biblical patterns and strategies that we have used to build our marriage and raise our children, who are now adults serving with us in the ministry.

We Give Up to Go Up

Not only do we need to learn to pray that God will deliver us from temptation and evil, but we also need to develop lifestyles that don't have us hanging out with temptation and evil! Rather than asking for deliverance from evil and temptation, why not avoid them altogether? If we are going to move forward into the blessings of God, there are some choices we have to make in our lifestyles. Saying yes to something means saying no to something else. But remember, anything that we give up for the Lord He will multiply back into our lives. We give up to go up! This is yet another chance for a divine exchange.

> CONVICTION FROM GOD IS ALWAYS FOR THE PURPOSE OF LIFTING US TO A HIGHER LEVEL. IT'S NEVER TO CONDEMN US OR EMBARRASS US.

Before we go any further, let me reiterate some things. God's conviction is always for the purpose of lifting us to a higher level. It's never to condemn us or embarrass us. Remember, the Lord is not pointing a finger of accusation at us; He is reaching out a hand to help us. As long as we're on this earth, He challenges us to pursue higher levels of faith and godliness. So, never feel condemned about where you are at any given time; be excited about where God is taking you! Your life is a journey, and from glory to glory, He's changing you!

Have you ever watched small children learning to walk? They teeter and totter and stumble and fall down, over and over again, until they finally master their balance and coordination. Their parents don't condemn or scold them as they're learning; rather, they encourage their children and cheer them on. Then, once the children learn to walk, the parents don't rebuke them for not knowing how to run. There is a natural progression to learning and growing. Children learn first to crawl, then to walk, and finally to run. At this point, they can pick up skipping, jumping, and playing sports. Of course, there are times when parents have to nudge their children ahead and keep them on a progressive course.

The progression of our spiritual growth isn't all that different. Step-by-step, level to level, from glory to glory, we should be growing and maturing. As we advance to each new accomplishment, our heavenly Father encourages us and cheers us on like a father clapping for his daughter when she takes her first steps. As we're mastering walking, He isn't condemning us or rebuking us for not having progressed immediately to running. If we stumble, He's not going to condemn us or kick us when we're down. Just as a good earthly father would be, our heavenly Father is proud of us and actively assists us with our spiritual growth and maturation. And not only that, but He and all of the angels of heaven also are actively cheering us on!

As a loving Father, He is committed to seeing us do our best and enter into His best. He continually challenges us to grow in order to take us to new levels of His blessings. His goal is to steer us away from danger areas and lead us into blessing areas. That's what the Ten Commandments, or the Law, are all about.

The Jewish book of law, the Torah, is named for a word that means "path." It's the pathway to all of God's blessings. Like a lit path in the night that shows us the way to go, the law is a clear path that takes us on the most direct route with the shortest distance to where we want to go. It's the path with the fewest pitfalls and least amounts of pain and heartache possible; the path that will lead you to the greatest amount of joy, peace, and happiness possible! How can we go wrong? I can say with complete confidence and experience that God's ways are the best ways!

Today's Choices Determine Tomorrow's Destiny

However, the Lord has given each of us a free will. His desire is for us to love Him and serve Him because we *choose* to do so, not because He forces us to. That wouldn't be true love! We can each make the choice to ignore God's path and try to create our own paths. We can choose to mess around with sin, hang out with the wrong people and in the wrong places, stumble around, mess up our reputations, and wreak havoc in our hearts

GOD WILL SPEAK TO US OR LEAD US THROUGH HIS WORD, AND THEN WE HAVE A CHOICE TO EITHER ACCEPT OR REJECT HIS DIRECTION. THE CHOICES THAT WE MAKE EACH DAY DETERMINE THE NEXT LEVEL TO WHICH GOD CAN TAKE US.

and lives, not to mention in the lives of others. We can choose to take the long, hard, winding road, or we can stay on the right path and make a beeline to all of God's goodness and blessings! The outcome really depends on the choices we make along the way.

Our long-term decisions and short-term choices alike have far-reaching consequences. Today's choices determine tomorrow's destiny!

There's God's part, and then there's our part. God will speak to us or lead us through His Word, and then we have a choice to either accept or reject His direction. The choices that we make each day determine the next level to which God can take us. And so, He challenges us and convicts us—not to condemn us but to lead us into abundant life, because He desires to give us life more abundantly in every area of our lives. Choose God. Choose His best. Choose life!

Avoiding the Enemy's Traps

Let's talk about a few ways in which the enemy tries to entice us or ensnare us in sinful behavior. The devil's schemes are often similar to the Burmese monkey trap, used by certain tribes in Myanmar. The tribesmen hollow out a coconut, leaving a tiny opening at one end, and then place some peanuts or other tasty items inside. They attach the coconut to a tree, where it's visible to the monkey. The monkey sees the food inside and reaches in to grab his treasure, clenching it tightly with his fist. However, while the tiny hole is big enough for the monkey to stick its hand into, it's too small for the monkey to be able to remove its hand while its fist is still clenched. If the monkey would simply let go of the treat, it could easily pull its hand back out. But the nature of the monkey is to stubbornly refuse to let go of its tasty treasure, and so it remains ensnared in the trap and becomes vulnerable to hunters. The animal's own stubborn will causes it to become a victim of its captors.

This is the same strategy that the devil uses in our lives to lay traps for us. We focus our attention on some attractive object, person, or activity that we consider to be a great treasure, and then we stubbornly clench our fists and minds around it, thereby becoming ensnared and trapped. Like the monkey, if we would just let go of our "treasure" and surrender to God, we would find our freedom.

> EVERY TIME YOU SAY YES TO GOD AND LET GO OF SOMETHING SINFUL OR HARMFUL, YOU OPEN A DOOR TO INCREDIBLE BLESSINGS AND MIRACLES.

If we will allow Him to, God will empower us with the ability to turn away from and be free from our bondage in order to turn toward His best. When we take an honest look at the things on which we place great value, we'll likely realize that they aren't worth risking our futures or our souls over. Every time you say yes to God and let go of something sinful or harmful, you open a door to incredible blessings and miracles. Let me say it again: there is a miracle on the other side of your obedience! There are also abundant blessings, unfathomable joy, and endless fulfillment on the other side of our obedience.

As I said before, the Lord doesn't condemn us, but He continually challenges us to move to new, higher levels. In praying, *"Lead us not into temptation,"* we're asking Him to give us the strength to stay away from and to overcome temptations. Let me repeat that the Lord does not *cause* trials or temptations to come into our lives, but He will *use* these situations to cause us to grow, mature, and become stronger.

Fleeing from Sin

In 1 Corinthians 10:13–14, Paul wrote that God will deliver us from temptation, but he also warned us to flee idolatry. Our deliverance is twofold: there's God's part, and then there's our part. God will help us and strengthen us from within, but we have to choose godly thoughts, words, and actions.

On the *Flip Wilson Show*, one of comedian Flip Wilson's characters, Geraldine, was always getting into trouble, and she was famous for the line, "The devil made me do it!" We're often tempted to use that phrase or similar excuses: "The devil tempted me. I tried to overcome, but he just made me do it!" Yes, the enemy will tempt us, but the choice is ours.

In Larry's teachings about the seven places Jesus shed His blood, he explains that one of the purposes for which Jesus shed His blood was to buy back our willpower. He writes,

> The first place Jesus shed His blood was in the garden of Gethsemane on the night of the Last Supper with His disciples. It's not a coincidence that the first place Jesus ransomed us or shed His redemptive blood was in a garden, because the first place we lost the power of God's blessing was in another garden, the garden of Eden....I've heard people say, "I have no willpower. I want to stop overeating, smoking, losing my temper (or whatever it is in their life that is out of control), but I have no willpower." We lost our willpower to do what is right, to do what is best for us, to do what is healthy, and to do what will bring benefit and blessing when Adam disobeyed God in the garden of Eden. Eve was deceived by the serpent, but Adam willfully disobeyed God. In other words, Eve was deceived by Satan, but Adam made a choice to disobey God.
>
> God had told Adam and Eve, "All in the garden is yours except the Tree of the Knowledge of Good and Evil." (See Genesis 3:17.) In essence, Adam said, "Father, not Your will, but mine be done," and at that moment, Adam sacrificed man's willpower in every area. With Adam's disobedience, we gave our will over to the enemy and lost our ability to say yes to all the good God has for us and no to all the bad the enemy wants to do to us. The willpower we lost in the garden of Eden was won back in the garden of Gethsemane when Jesus said, "Not My will, but Thy will be done." (See Matthew 26:39.)[8]

Through the power of the blood of Jesus, we do have the willpower to overcome temptation, sin, and evil!

---

[8] Huch, *Free at Last*, 109–110.

At one time or another, we've all thought or said something like, "Well, I just can't change," or "I couldn't help myself," or "I tried to change, but it's no use." The truth is, now that we are Christians, those old excuses don't hold up anymore! The Holy Spirit lives within each of us, empowering us to keep from doing the wrong thing and equipping us to do the right thing! All we have to do is allow the Holy Spirit to guide us and enable us to make the right choices. Remember that *we are more than conquerors through him that loved us* (Romans 8:37)!

> THE HOLY SPIRIT LIVES WITHIN EACH OF US, EMPOWERING US TO KEEP FROM DOING THE WRONG THING AND ALSO EQUIPPING US TO DO THE RIGHT THING!

Larry and I both like to tell the story of the little boy who kept sneaking down to the river to go swimming. His dad told him, "I don't want you swimming in that river anymore. You could get hurt. You could drown. It's too dangerous." The little boy promised his dad that he would stay away from the river. The next day, his dad decided to check on his son. When he drove by the river, sure enough, there was his son swimming away! The dad marched down to the riverbank and shouted, "I told you not to go swimming in this river! What do you think you're doing, young man?" The little boy said, "I'm sorry, Dad. I didn't mean to. I really didn't mean to." His dad replied, "If you didn't mean to, then why did you bring your swimming trunks?"

Just like that little boy, we can try to plead our cases, saying, "I just couldn't help myself," or "I didn't mean to." But the same question applies to us: why did we bring our swimming trunks? Why do we plan and prepare ourselves to go to the places where we know we shouldn't be with the people we know we shouldn't be with?

The Bible is full of warnings about the need to overcome temptation. In 2 Timothy 2:22, Paul urged us to *flee the evil desires of youth* (NIV), and in 1 Corinthians 6:18, he said, *Flee from sexual immorality* (NIV). In other words, "Don't be hanging out in places where this type of behavior is the

> WE NEED TO MAKE UP OUR MINDS AND SET OUR BOUNDARIES BEFORE WE'RE FACED WITH TEMPTATION.

norm, and don't hang out with people who regularly practice it!" It is foolish to put ourselves in environments of temptation and then make the excuse that we couldn't help ourselves.

We need to make up our minds and set our boundaries *before* we're faced with temptation. We need to avoid even putting ourselves into situations with the potential to lure us into sinful behaviors and wrong choices. We *can* avoid temptation successfully by avoiding the wrong people and places. Have I gone from ministering to meddling yet? If so, it's only because I want God's best for you! Often, the most difficult choices bring the greatest blessings.

We can rationalize all we want, but the truth is that each of us has a conscience that speaks loud and clear. The question is whether we will pay attention to it or ignore it. Remember, God always has our best interests in mind! If you have decided to trust Him with the future in terms of eternal life, you can certainly trust Him with the future in terms of your earthly, natural life, too. He is a good and loving Father. Choose the best and let Him do the rest!

I know that we all desire the blessings of God in our lives, but we need to realize that His blessings don't come automatically. There are certain things we have to do to line ourselves up with the will and the promises of God in order to receive His blessings. We serve a good God who isn't a ruthless, judgmental taskmaster. But there are some boundaries, guidelines, and restrictions that we need to live by. There is a path that we have to stay on. The following guidelines will keep you on the proper path.

Avoid Toxic Relationships

I grew up in a great, loving family. We weren't extremely well-versed in Christian truth, but we were pretty moralistic, compared to most people. Yet when I was saved, I had to make some choices. And some of those choices included leaving behind old friends who were toxic and had been dragging me down and drawing me back into the world and away from

God and church. I had to cut loose some good friends and longtime relationships. I had to make some lifestyle changes, which also meant making some relationship and influence changes.

Saying yes to God often means saying no to other people, hobbies, habits, and activities in your life. When you make a decision that necessitates cutting certain relationships and activities from your life, it may initially seem like you're going to be deprived of something or someone you value and care about. But that decision will have a lasting impact on the path of your life—and for the better. Always remember that with God, you give up to go up.

Another way of putting this is the old saying, "For every death, there's a resurrection." When I was a new Christian, I read a Scripture that changed my life. It was Matthew 16:25, where Jesus said, *"For whosoever will save his life shall lose it: and whosoever will lose his life for my sake shall find it."* I remember reading this for the first time and realizing that if I tried to create my own path of happiness according to the world's standards, I would lose out on what God had for me in the Word! If, however, I would let go of all the worldly aims and pleasures from my past, I would find all that God had prepared for me to enjoy in my future. It came down to a choice to believe either the promises of the world or the promises of the Word. At that moment, I chose to trust God with my future. I chose to "let go and let God."

In hindsight, I think it's apparent that I made the right choice! Let me encourage you to make the right choice to trust God with your future, just as I did more than thirty years ago. I never could have imagined, let alone created, the incredibly wonderful life of blessings that the Lord had in store for me. An incredibly wonderful life of blessings awaits you, too!

> THERE IS A MIRACLE ON THE OTHER SIDE OF THEIR OBEDIENCE. ACTUALLY, IT'S MORE LIKE A NEVER-ENDING SEA OF MIRACLES!

I like to tell people that there is a miracle on the other side of their obedience. Actually, it's more like a never-ending sea of miracles! Say this out loud with me right now: "It's my time for a new beginning!"

Develop and Maintain a Penitent Heart
and a Humble Attitude

When we choose to become Christians, a few or many of our former habits need to change. Some issues are blatant and need to be dealt with right away. Other things may be less obvious but are brought to our attention as we mature in the faith. Regardless of the habits we need to change and the rate at which we realize this, the key is to develop and maintain a penitent heart and a humble attitude.

Learn to welcome and embrace personal growth, because it is always followed by great personal blessings! And remember, from glory to glory, He is changing us, taking us to higher levels, and shaping us more and more into His image!

Realize That Sin Doesn't Satisfy for Long

We're all going to face various temptations over time. There will usually be a situation, activity, or relationship that appeals to you or looks enticing but is actually a diversion, dead end, or trap. We can choose to go down those little side roads of diversion, explore all kinds of bizarre things, and get involved in lots of wild and crazy stuff. It might be fun for a while, for even the Bible acknowledges the *"pleasures of sin"* (Hebrews 11:25); however, this verse makes the important distinction that these pleasures last only *"for a season."* There will always be a price to pay! The enemy of our souls is extremely clever, and he knows exactly how to appeal to each of us individually. Just like a spider, he can spin a web of deception without our notice, and before we know it, we've become ensnared in his sticky net. Each wrong choice leads us deeper and deeper into the entrapment of the enemy.

Dethrone Yourself

One of the problems with society today is that we've become short-sighted to the point where we don't look at the big picture. We don't project down the road of life and evaluate the probable long-term consequences of our actions. Many people have been raised in a culture of self-centeredness and entitlement; they just think, say, and do whatever feels good to them at any given time. We have been molded by society and the media to be consumed with self-centeredness and self-absorption to the point where we have little regard for the welfare of others, especially as concerns our effect on them. We don't like to admit it, but most of us live by the motto, "It's all about me!"

We have been conditioned to think that everything the world has to offer should be available to us personally. In this era of entitlement, we want to—no, *deserve* to—have it all. The world owes us.

> WHEN SELF IS ON THE THRONE OF YOUR LIFE, YOU CAN NEVER GET ENOUGH PLEASURE, ENOUGH STUFF, ENOUGH ATTENTION, ENOUGH MONEY, OR ENOUGH SATISFACTION.

The truth is that this belief is a bottomless pit. When self is on the throne of your life, you can never get enough pleasure, enough stuff, enough attention, enough money, or enough satisfaction. The more you try to pour into the bottomless pit, the less satisfied you end up feeling. As the foundation of your life spreads wide but remains shallow, you become emptied of genuine feelings and desensitized to anything truly meaningful. You ultimately come to a place where nothing means much and everything lacks significance. You find yourself feeling ripped off and thinking that there must be more to life. You'll be right about that, but the "more to life" is hard to experience when you've given away your heart, mind, and body in exchange for passing pleasures and temporary delights.

As I've said before, saying yes to God means saying no to certain things—but the point isn't self-deprivation! Rather, the point is to protect us and to move us into the blessings of God. So, let's not be shortsighted. Let's commit to making wise choices based on our assessments of what awaits us on the road ahead. Let's stop and think about the decisions we're making. Before making a decision, always ask yourself, *While I might feel like doing this today, will I regret this in the days and years to come?*

Living in Deliverance from Evil

Someone once said, "Our life is God's gift to us. What we do with it is our gift back to Him." We need to take ownership of and responsibility for our choices and our futures. Again, Proverbs 4:23 says, *"Keep your heart with all diligence, for out of it spring the issues of life"* (NKJV). We need to be picky about what we let into our minds and spirits, because whatever we permit to enter will profoundly affect our decision-making. "Garbage in, garbage out" is a succinct summary of Jesus' point in Matthew 12:34–35:

> *How can you who are evil say anything good? For out of the overflow of the heart the mouth speaks. The good man brings good things out of the good stored up in him, and the evil man brings evil things out of the evil stored up in him.* (NIV)

We live in a real world, and we can never be completely isolated from its influences, even if we are especially careful about our associations and pastimes. We do have the ability, however, to choose how those influences affect us.

In order to counteract the world's sinful influences and resist its insidious temptations, we have to maintain a primary focus on God. This comes through committing time to prayer, studying the Word and letting its wisdom take root in our hearts, and developing intimate relationships with God Himself.

Think about this: by saying no to certain things, you are opening yourself up to unlimited access to God Almighty! He has promised us that everything we give up for Him, He will multiply back to us. In Luke 18:29–30, Jesus told His disciples about the reward for giving one's life to follow Him, saying, *"No one who has left home or wife or brothers or parents or children for the sake of the kingdom of God will fail to receive many times as much in this age and, in the age to come, eternal life"* (NIV). We have these additional assurances from the apostle Paul:

> *Whoever sows sparingly will also reap sparingly, and whoever sows generously will also reap generously....Now he who supplies seed to the sower and bread for food will also supply and increase your store of seed and will enlarge the harvest of your righteousness. You will be*

made rich in every way so that you can be generous on every occasion,
and through us your generosity will result in thanksgiving to God.

(2 Corinthians 9:6, 10–11 NIV)

So, let's take our focus off of what we're missing out on and refocus on all of the outrageous miracles and blessings that are in store for us!

It is also important that we surround ourselves with godly influences by becoming involved with a Bible-believing church, associating with fellow Christians, and hearing faith-filled messages on a regular basis.

The Holy Spirit Empowers Us to Resist Temptation and Overcome Generational Curses

The most amazing part of all is that when it comes to overcoming temptation, you aren't just out there on your own. That's what the power of the Holy Spirit is all about! It's not about you somehow mustering the inner strength to resist every temptation known to man. First of all, when we truly meet the Lord, He gives us an entirely new "want-to-do" list. Then, through prayer, we are able to tap into the equipping power of the Holy Spirit and stand strong against the attacks of the enemy and the temptations of the world.

Furthermore, we can break the power of generational or family curses over our lives and over the lives of our loved ones. My husband's book *Free at Last* is highly recommended reading for in-depth teaching on how to break these curses. If you've read Larry's testimony, you found out that when he was saved, he was immediately delivered from years of alcohol and drug addictions. He didn't just *decide* to change his old habits; he was *delivered* and *set free* from them, never again to crave alcohol, cigarettes, or drugs! He experienced true and genuine deliverance.

That's the miracle of the power of God. We don't have to *try* not to sin. We don't have to *try* to stay on the right course every day. We don't have to *try* to muster enough willpower and strength to hold on and keep our heads above water, spiritually. Larry and I have learned how to break the curses over our lives, and we can teach you how to break the curses over your life, too!

A True Story of Miraculous Deliverance

In our ministry, Larry and I have had the exciting privilege of seeing thousands of people set free from bondages, addictions, and dysfunctional lifestyles. What the Lord has done for us we are committed to seeing Him do for others!

In our first church in Santa Fe, New Mexico, we saw thousands of troubled youths give their lives to the Lord and be set free from drug and alcohol addictions and violence. Many of these young people came from homes filled with addictions, anger, and abuse. Many of them had fathers, mothers, brothers, and sisters who were in prison; many had themselves been in and out of juvenile detention centers. Even at their young ages, these kids were headed down a destructive path. But by the grace of God, we were able to break the vicious cycles and turn many of their lives around.

I remember our first encounter with several of these young people. We had rented a tiny building, formerly Henry's Meat and Liquor Market, to be our church, and it was located in the heart of the worst neighborhood in town. In Spanish, this neighborhood was referred to as the *Barrios*, and it was the area where all the gangs hung out. In fact, our parking lot was the main rendezvous for drug deals and all related activities. Weeks before we moved in, there had been a shoot-out on the front doorstep of our building in which several teenage gang members were killed.

On the night before our grand opening, we worked frantically to transform the little building from a meat and liquor market into a house of God! We threw down some cheap carpet to cover the worn concrete floors, nailed faux wood paneling to the walls, constructed a small platform, tried to plug the leaks in the ceiling, painted over the vile graffiti on the outside of the building, and scrubbed the smoke film off the insides of the windows. (We couldn't scrub the outsides of the windows because they were covered with protective iron bars!) We converted the back liquor storeroom into a nursery and the meat locker/walk-in cooler into a pastor's office.

We also put the finishing touches on our brand-new sanctuary, adorning the platform with a homemade pulpit and setting up an electric keyboard for me to play, all the while praising God for His amazing grace. The Bible says, *"Do not despise this small beginning"* (Zechariah 4:10 TLB), and we certainly heeded this verse. Whatever we lacked in style we made up for in enthusiasm! We were so full of zeal and anticipation that we nearly burst! Our dream was not to create a gorgeous, elegant cathedral; our dream was to create a place where lives would be changed!

Around three in the morning, we were taking down the last of the neon beer signs when the front door opened and in burst some teenage boys. They were obviously inebriated, and we were unsure of their intentions. We were aware that the building had been the recent target of multiple robberies.

The boys mockingly asked what we were doing, and we told them that we were opening a church. They sneered menacingly, and while Larry wasn't at all intimidated, I certainly was! Even so, we began to talk to them. We shared Larry's testimony and told them about God's love.

By four o'clock, they all were weeping and praying with us and had committed to be the head ushers for opening night! They even helped us finish cleaning out the church, on the condition that they could take the neon beer signs—another divine exchange!

Those young men became like our own sons. They were totally delivered of their addictions, bondages, and violent ways. They went on to become the most committed and loyal leaders of our church; they were among the most radical soulwinners you've ever seen. Instead of bringing terror to the streets, they brought the gospel to the streets! With these young men by our side, we evangelized many neighborhoods and saw thousands of young people saved, de- livered, and drastically changed!

> THE YOUNG PEOPLE WERE TRANSFORMED FROM JUVENILE DELINQUENTS TO GOD-LOVING, BIGHEARTED, HARDWORKING, PRODUCTIVE YOUNG MEN AND WOMEN!

Before we met them, the young people of these neighborhoods had seen, done, and en- countered it all—everything, that is, except for the love of God and the transforming power of the Holy Spirit. In addition, most of them had never experienced love and acceptance from another person. As Larry and I—and the Lord—reached out to them, surrounded them with love, and believed in them, they were transformed from juvenile delinquents to God-loving, bighearted, hardworking, productive young men and women! Their lives were changed so dynamically that the local newspapers printed several feature articles about them, and the courts were actually sentencing kids with similar backgrounds to the custody of Larry and me and our church! Several of the ex-gang members, young men and women alike, received the Governor's Award for the Most Changed Life. Many of them went on into full-time ministry and are to this day reaching others with the love and power of God.

As you can tell by this testimony, when we break a curse, we're not just breaking the act of sin. We're also breaking the *iniquity* behind that sin, which is the driving force within us that causes us to want to commit those sins. In many cases, those iniquities and tendencies are passed from one generation to the next, continuing and perpetuating negative patterns.

Many of you reading this book know exactly what we're talking about. You know all too well the often unfortunate truth of the phrases, "Like father, like son. Like mother, like daughter."

Those driving forces, those addictive personalities, and those negative behavior patterns are passed on from one generation to the next. But they don't have to persist!

THROUGH PRAYER, WE CAN BREAK EVERY STRONGHOLD AND CURSE AND THEN LIVE IN THE FREEDOM OF GOD. WE CAN MOVE FORWARD AND FACE FEWER TEMPTATIONS EVERY DAY.

We can break those bondages and strongholds once and for all. Again, *iniquity* is both the sin and the force inside of us that drives us to commit that sin. Thank the Lord that this is exactly what our Savior died for—to break the curses over our lives; to sever the roots that drive us to act in negative, harmful, destructive ways! Whether we have an affinity for anger, violence, addiction, depression, or another issue, thanks be to God that we can break those strongholds, tendencies, and bondages once and for all! We can sever those ties through the blood of our Savior, Jesus Christ, whose death and resurrection made it possible for us to think, talk, and act differently than others in the world around us. You may have been a drug addict. You may have been an alcoholic. You may have been all kinds of other things. But you are completely free of those identities when you break the curses in your life. Through prayer, we can break every stronghold and curse and then live in the freedom of God. We can move forward and face fewer temptations every day.

Larry doesn't call himself a "recovering addict"; he calls himself a "delivered ex-addict." We truly can be brand-new people through the cleansing blood of Jesus Christ.

The Set-Apart Life

Never sell yourself short or jeopardize your future by lowering your standards. You are a child of God with an incredible, God-designed destiny ahead of you! Always take the high road. The Lord has a specific plan of destiny, a path of purpose, and a place of blessing for each of us. We must continually value our relationships and right standing with the Lord above our relationships with others. People will come and go, and events will begin and end, but a relationship with God will last forever. As a matter of fact, it will last throughout all eternity!

You and I have been set apart! The psalmist praised God for this marvelous fact, saying, *"You created my inmost being; you knit me together in my mother's womb. I praise you because I am fearfully and wonderfully made; your works are wonderful, I know that full well"* (Psalm 139:13–14 NIV). We are not ordinary or run-of-the-mill; we are special and unique! We are to live our lives set apart from the masses—thinking, talking, and behaving in ways that differ from the godless norm. Our lives are to attain a higher level of godliness and faith. In a world of billions, you and I are privileged to be called chosen ones—not because we're better than everybody else, but because we're different: we love God and choose to follow Him.

Jesus told His disciples—and this applies to us, too—that *"if the world hates you, keep in mind that it hated me first. If you belonged to the world, it would love you as its own. As it is, you do not belong to the world, but I have* **chosen** *you out of the world. That is why the world hates you"* (John 15:18–19 NIV, emphasis added). And in 1 Peter 2:9, we are called *"a* **chosen people**, *a royal priesthood, a holy nation, a people belonging to God, that you may declare*

WE SHOULD NEVER SETTLE FOR A COMMON, ORDINARY, DULL EXISTENCE, FOR OUR LORD HAS AN EXTRAORDINARY PLAN, PURPOSE, AND DESTINY FOR EACH OF US THAT IS GREATER THAN ANYTHING WE COULD DREAM OF.

the praises of him who called you out of darkness into his wonderful light" (NIV, emphasis added).

We have the incredible honor and privilege to know, commune with, and represent God on the earth. We should never settle for a common, ordinary, dull existence, for our Lord has an extraordinary plan, purpose, and destiny for each of us that is greater than anything we could dream of. Let's choose to live as people set apart for special purposes!

Get Ready to Pray!

Okay, let's get ready to pray together. When we pray with this new level of understanding about our authority as believers to overcome sin, we will come out different! I don't believe that we have to spend the entirety of our time in prayer begging the Lord to help us and trying to convince Him of how hard our situations are. Let's get past all of that and move forward. Let's start reaping positive results in our lives. Let's take dominion, pull down strongholds, break some generational curses, and block the strategies of the enemy. Then, how about letting God use us to break some strongholds that are in the world around us—in our friends and families, in our schools, in our neighborhoods, in our cities, in our governments, and in our nations? Put your foot down in the spiritual realm and turn some things around in your life, as well as in the lives of those whom you know and love!

Let's Pray!

Father, we thank You and praise You for Your goodness and love. We thank You for the blood of Jesus, which cleanses us and covers us. We thank You for the power of the Holy Spirit, who lives within us and empowers us to live above all sin, evil, and temptation. We thank You for calling us to be more than conquerors through Jesus Christ, who loves us.

Lord, we know that You are never condemning us or pointing a finger of accusation at us, but that You are reaching out a hand to help us. From glory to glory, You are changing us and molding us more into Your image; You are lifting us to new and higher levels, and You are working Your will in us, for us, and through us.

Lord, we ask You to lead us away from all temptation and deliver us from all evil. Give us the will, determination, and strength to say no to the world and yes to Your will. We stand on Your promises that You have given us in Your Word that as we surrender to Your will, You will shower us with peace, joy, and abundant blessings.

Right now, we bind every force of darkness, every stronghold of addiction, and every evil temptation in our lives. We rebuke the influences of the enemy and of the world. We stand in agreement that every curse is broken over our lives, our children, our spouses, and our families. We claim that every curse of bondage and every stronghold is broken through the blood of Jesus Christ. We claim the blood of Jesus to cleanse our hearts, minds, and physical bodies.

We acknowledge that even though we live in a world full of ungodliness and temptation, You have called us and empowered us to rise above these negative forces with dominion and authority. Right now, we stand against every plan of the enemy for our minds, our lives, and our families. Every demonic stronghold is defeated and broken. Every plan of the enemy is cancelled in our lives, in our minds, in our futures, and in our children. Every spirit that tries to drive us to the world—to addictions, to sinful temptations—is broken and bound. Every spirit of iniquity is severed through the blood of Jesus Christ. We proclaim that the enemy is under our feet.

Father, we put our feet down. There will be no stronghold that can hold our minds or our futures captive. Father, we take dominion over every spirit that would try to influence us or drive us away from Your plans and Your will.

Father, we ask You to put a hedge of protection around our minds, our spirits, and our bodies. No stronghold or weapon that is formed against us shall prosper. We commit our lives afresh to You. Lord, we commit our minds to be havens for Your Word. Father, sanctify our minds. Place a spirit of righteousness within each of us. Give us hearts after Your own heart; create in us clean hearts that hunger for You and Your Word.

Father, right now, we call in our family members, including our children and grandchildren, to salvation and wholeness. We break every evil spirit and demonic stronghold that would try to grip their minds. We command every influence from the enemy to be broken and severed through the blood of Jesus Christ. We claim their souls. We claim their hearts for You. Cleanse them by the blood of Jesus, and let the Holy Spirit draw them back to You. We know that no name can stand above the name of Jesus Christ, and so no spirit of sin or addiction can grip their minds. These spirits are bound through the blood and authority of Jesus Christ.

Father, release Your Spirit upon the hearts and minds of our family members, including our children and grandchildren. We know that these curses are broken and reversed, and so, Lord, we release upon ourselves and our family members renewed minds. Father, every demonic stronghold is broken. Where there was hatred, God, replace it with love. Where there is rebellion, God, replace it with submission. Where there has been sin and iniquity, replace them with wholeness and purity. Where there has been unrighteousness, God, replace it with integrity, righteousness, honesty, and pure thoughts. Where there has been doubt and fears, Father, replace them with faith, hope, and positive thoughts of You.

Heavenly Father, deliver us from evil and empower us to resist the temptations of the devil. In Jesus' name we pray, amen.

PRAYER AND PROMISE PRINCIPLES

- The Lord came to bring us life—and more abundantly!
- Serving God is not just a bunch of do's and don'ts. It's a bunch of get-to's, opportunities, and privileges!

- Anything that we give up for the Lord He will multiply back into our lives. We give up to go up!

- Every time you say yes to God and let go of something sinful or harmful, you open a door to incredible blessings and miracles.

- Through prayer, we are able to tap into the equipping power of the Holy Spirit and stand strong against the attacks of the enemy and the temptations of the world.

- The Lord has a specific plan of destiny, a path of purpose, and a place of blessing for each of us!

Chapter Nineteen

FOR THINE IS THE KINGDOM, AND THE POWER, AND THE GLORY, FOR EVER

The Lord's Prayer ends just as it begins—by giving praise, glory, and honor to God. We should always conclude our prayers by acknowledging God as the King of Kings and Lord of Lords, the sovereign Creator and Ruler of all things, whose kingdom will endure forever. In acknowledging His sovereignty, we show that we're trusting Him to hear our prayers and to deal with our affairs according to His wonderful, divine will.

Right now, let's take the time to give God the glory for the amazing things He's done in our lives, as well as in the lives of the following individuals who discovered the power of praying God's promises. As you learn to take ownership of His promises through prayer, you will see miracles manifest in your life, too.

Carl Walks Again

Our church witnessed an outrageous miracle of healing in the lives of a couple who have been faithfully attending our church for several years. The husband, Carl, had been in a due to an injury he sustained years earlier. He and his wife, Christie, chased me down to tell me what happened. Listen to the story of what the Lord has done for them!

More than thirteen years ago, Carl injured his back on a job. Three of the discs in his lower back were crushed. Over the years, the injuries and the pain became increasingly severe and debilitating to the point that he ended up in a wheelchair full-time. A specialist had placed a device in his back to help to ease the pain but without much effect. Carl and Christie had been standing continually in faith for his miracle. They were (and are) so faithful in church attendance, never missing a service, and are committed tithers and givers. In the past year, they have seen financial miracles time and time again, including a $77,000 debt cancellation of a past medical bill!

The greatest miracle so far, though, came about a month ago. As I was chatting with several people in the hallway before church, I suddenly heard a voice shouting excitedly, "Pastor Tiz! Look what the Lord has done for Carl!" I looked over to see Carl walking toward me! He was using a cane to help support his weak legs, but he was walking on his own! Well, needless to say, we all had a "Hallelujah Fit"!

> AS HE MADE THE EFFORT TO STAND, GOD POURED STRENGTH INTO HIS BODY, AND HE STOOD AND BEGAN TO TAKE STEPS.

Carl and Christie had been believing for and dreaming of this day for a long time, and that morning, Carl had simply awakened and thought, *Today is the day for the manifestation of my miracle.* He decided to step out in faith and take hold of God's healing power. He grabbed a cane and tried to stand up. At first, it was a struggle, as his legs were very weak from the years he'd spent in his wheelchair. But as he made the effort to stand, God poured strength into his body, and he stood and began to take steps. With every step and each new day, he has grown stronger and more stable. Not only that, but his pain has subsided greatly! What an incredible testimony of how great our God is! If the Lord can do this for Carl, imagine what He can do for you!

Laura's Pain Miraculously Disappears

A woman named Laura had recently begun coming to our church when she fell and twisted her ankle and wrist. For two months, the doctors couldn't pinpoint the source of her pain in either area. They put her on strong pain medication to ease her pain and hoped for improvement. However, over time, the pain did not fade away, but rather worsened as it spread from her ankle to her toes and all the way up to her hip. Her wrist became so inflamed that the doctor put it in a wrist brace. They also gave Laura an air cast for her ankle.

Being pretty new to the faith message, Laura didn't really know much about believing for a miracle. One Sunday morning, though, as she sat in agonizing pain and listened to Larry's message, hope and faith began to fill her soul. At the end of the service, she asked for prayer for a miracle healing. As she left the sanctuary afterward, she could feel the pain easing up but was almost afraid to hope for too much.

By the time she arrived at home later that afternoon, Laura realized that she was long overdue for her usual dose of painkiller medication. But as she walked around her home, she felt no pain in her wrist or her ankle. So, she took off her brace and air cast to see if that made any difference.

Laura told me that she felt absolutely no pain! Still cautious, she thought, *Okay, great, but let's see how I feel in the morning.* She took no medication that evening but went to bed hoping for the best.

When Laura awakened on Monday morning, she immediately got up and tested her wrist and ankle for pain. She began to weep with joy as she confirmed that there was still no pain whatsoever to be found! One week later, she ran to me to report that not one trace of pain had returned to her body! Laura has been totally and forever convinced of the healing power of our God!

Jenny and Jim See Their Marriage Restored

I received a letter from a couple telling me their story of how the Lord had restored their broken marriage. They had been invited to our church repeatedly by their neighbors, and after about a year of this, they reluctantly agreed to come just to get their neighbors to quit bothering them with their "religion." Neither Jenny nor Jim had ever spent much time in a church, and they basically knew nothing about Christianity.

Their life together hadn't always been blissful. Eight years before they started coming to church, they began dating as young adults. Within a few months, Jenny became pregnant, and they married—not out of love but out of obligation. Within a short period of time, their relationship grew very hostile. Tension, mutual resentment, and financial stress began to domi-nate most of their days. Then the baby came, compounding the chaos. Without planning to, Jenny became pregnant again within a few months. The couple was just barely hanging onto their strife-filled marriage. After a few years of unhappiness, they made the decision to divorce.

Jenny and Jim separated and started the legal proceedings. One day, Jenny was feeling terribly sad about the condition of their lives, and she was especially guilt-ridden about the effect her divorce would have on her children. She mourned their impending loss of a stable family environ-ment and the fact that the children would likely suffer the most from the mess. She felt completely hopeless and helpless.

> SHE FELT FOR THE FIRST TIME IN HER LIFE THAT PERHAPS GOD WAS REAL AND DID CARE ABOUT HER AND HER FAMILY. AT THE ALTAR CALL, SHE GAVE HER LIFE TO THE LORD AND ASKED HIM TO HELP HER MARRIAGE TO BECOME SOMETHING BEAUTIFUL.

About this time, their neighbor "hap-pened" to drop by and invited them to church. Even though Jenny had no desire to go to church and had no clue that it could provide the answer to her mess, she took her children with her to church in order to ap-pease her neighbor.

From the moment Jenny walked into the church building, she said, hope and joy flooded her soul. As she heard the message, she felt for the first time in her life that per-haps God *was* real and *did* care about her and her family. At the altar call, she gave her life to the Lord and asked Him to help her mar-riage to become something beautiful. Peace and happiness overwhelmed her.

Much to Jenny's surprise, when she ar-rived home that afternoon, Jim was waiting outside the house. He told her that he want-ed to make things right, but that he didn't know how. Jenny shared with him what had just happened to her at our church and asked him to come with her on Wednesday night. He could see a big change in her attitude, and he agreed to go.

On that Wednesday night, Jim and Jenny came down to the altar, weeping and holding each other. They prayed together for the first time in their lives. The Holy Spirit poured over them and through them, and they sobbed and sobbed as the Lord gave them a new beginning. We prayed over them and broke every spirit of strife, division, and discord. We released the Lord's Spirit of healing and restoration. Jim and Jenny left that service holding hands and with huge smiles on their faces, and they went home *together* to start a new life!

From that moment on, their lives—and the life of their family—have never been the same! They enrolled in every class we had available on topics from marriage to raising children to biblical financial practices.

More than three years have passed since Jenny's desperate night, and I am happy to tell you that Jim and Jenny have a beautiful marriage and family. They recently shared with me that they had bought a new, wonderful home, Jim has earned several promotions, and their children are on the Honor Roll at school! The entire family is involved in leadership at our church. Their desire is to help others find the answers that they found more than three years ago in the God who heals and restores!

Tonya's World Is Rocked by the Word

Once, while teaching on prayer at our church in Dallas, I was amazed by the responses of many people. One woman named Tonya came and told me that learning to pray with authority and power had changed her life dramatically. She explained that she had been born and raised in church but had lost interest in her teenage years. To make a long story short, years later, she found herself as a thirty-year-old single mom trying to raise a beautiful little girl named Alicia. Tonya struggled to make ends meet, and she felt very alone as she tried to juggle all of the responsibilities of working and raising a daughter by herself. She told me that when a friend invited her to come to our church, she really wasn't interested because of her past experiences in churches.

She said that when she finally came, however, her world was "rocked"! She shared with me that in all of her years of attending church, she had never heard teachings that actually altered her lifestyle. No one had ever taught her how to pray with power, and the only times she prayed were in desperate situations, when she knew no more than to say, "God, help me." That had been the extent of her prayer life for almost thirty years!

Therefore, when she began to hear about all of the blessings and miracles that the Lord has made available through prayer, she said it felt like Christmas morning, for every time she prayed, she felt like she was opening a new gift! She started playing my prayer CD in the car every morning as she drove Alicia to school, and together, they prayed along with me. Each morning as they drove and had their morning power prayer time, they became more confident and bold in their faith. What had once been a boring, silent drive became the most exciting half hour of their day! Tonya even told me that on several mornings, she had tried to bypass the prayer time because she had too many things on her mind, but Alicia had always insisted she play the prayer CD, saying, "Mom, we have to get our prayer time in! We don't want to miss out on God's blessings for us today!"

MIRACLES BEGAN TO MANIFEST FOR HER AND HER DAUGHTER. AS THEIR PRAYERS BECAME INCREASINGLY SPECIFIC, THEY SAW GOD ANSWER THEM SPECIFICALLY!

The more Tonya came to church and was fed by our teachings, the more she felt empowered to step out in faith and into God's blessings! Her heart had become filled with hope, expectancy, and joy. Miracles began to manifest for her and her daughter. As their prayers became increasingly specific, they saw God answer them specifically! She got the new job that they had prayed for, along with the raise she wanted! Tonya and Alicia were able to move into a new house in a better neighborhood and school district.

Alicia grew in her own spiritual life, falling in love with the Lord and developing her own intimacy with Him. God poured out His blessings upon her, and she became happier than she had ever been. She and her mother grew united through the prayer times they shared together, and the emotional distance between them was closed.

Together, Tonya and Alicia have been experiencing the manifestation of God's help and miraculous favor in every area of their lives. To top it all off, Tonya said, "The best thing of all is that I know I'm not alone anymore!

I have genuine help from the Lord to make ends meet, to juggle everything, and to take care of and raise my little girl! And the changes in my daughter are nothing short of miraculous! She has come out of her shell and is so alive with joy, hope, and zeal for life! We wake up every morning in anticipation of what the Lord is going to do for us that day! We are aware of His presence throughout our entire day, and we look for daily opportunities for Him to use our lives to be blessings to others! We have never known such joy in our lives! Thank you for teaching us how to pray!"

Carl and Tina Learn the Secret of Breakthroughs

A family that had watched our television show *New Beginnings* for some time decided to move to Dallas in order to attend our church and hear our teachings year-round and in person. After about a month of being involved at our church, they wrote us a letter and told us their story.

The husband, Carl, wrote that he and his wife, Tina, had been Spirit-filled Christians for more than thirty-three years and had grown up going to church. He said they had been happy but continually faced struggles in their finances, as well as in other areas. They had prayed together about a year before moving to Dallas and had asked the Lord to give them a new beginning. Shortly after praying that prayer, they turned on their TV and saw our program for the first time. When they heard us say that the name of our church is New Beginnings, they knew that the Lord was leading them to move here to attend, and so they did just that!

In their letter, Carl and Tina told us that in the last three months of sitting under our ministry, their eyes had been opened to more truths than they had learned in the past thirty-three years! As they have taken ownership of the truths of Scripture and incorporated them into their lives, they have seen breakthroughs in their family, their business, and their finances. They said that they had never heard that so many blessings were available from the Lord. For the first time in their lives, they stood in boldness, confidence, and authority! They said that God truly had given them a new beginning.

Jenny Can Breathe Again

When a woman named Jenny came to one of our Freedom Encounters, she experienced an unexpected miracle. She later told me that she had come believing that the Lord would touch her heart and free her from years of emotional hurt and pain. She explained that when we prayed for her, she felt the burdens drop off, the baggage fall away, and joy flood her soul. She had never experienced anything like it before, and she was ecstatic about her newfound freedom.

But that wasn't all! She went on to tell me that she had been a heavy smoker for thirty-seven years. She had quit eight years prior to attending the Freedom Encounter because she had developed emphysema, and the serious lung disease had nearly taken her life. Her doctor had prescribed for her a bronchial inhaler, which she used six to seven times a day in order to breathe more easily. But Jenny said that even with the help of the inhaler, she still had a great deal of difficulty breathing deeply.

As we prayed that day for God to heal Jenny's broken heart, the Lord took it one step further and healed her damaged lungs! Jenny said that after our prayer, she took a deep breath of air, and it went way down into a place where she had not been able to get air to reach for a long time! Since that day, she has not had to use her inhaler at all. Jenny wept as she told me how the Lord had healed her broken heart and her damaged lungs. She said, "Wow! I had some Encounter!"

We serve such a great God, don't we?

Jeremy Turns His Life Around

One day, we received a letter from a man named Jeremy who had recently given his heart back to the Lord. He wrote that he had been brought up in a church but had left in search of fun, wild times. He went on to say that he had made a royal mess of not only his own life, but also the lives of his family members and other loved ones.

Jeremy felt like the prodigal son from the parable in Luke 15:11–32 when he turned on his TV one afternoon and saw my husband deliver his personal testimony on a Christian program. He prayed with Larry over the

TV and gave his heart back to the Lord. He then sent for some of Larry's teachings on DVD and began to saturate his mind and spirit with the messages of deliverance and restoration.

From that moment on, the Lord has been putting Jeremy's life back together. Jeremy has been set free from addictions to drugs and alcohol. He is holding down a great job and has purchased a beautiful home. He has a Christian girlfriend, and both of them are active in their church. Jeremy's relationships with his parents and other family members have been healed and restored.

Jeremy closed his letter by saying, "Thank you for sharing your testimony. When everyone else had given up on me, you gave me hope that my life was worth something. When I had given up on myself, you gave me direction to turn things around. When I felt that God was through with me, you showed me that He still loves a prodigal son. Words can never express how grateful I am for your pointing me back to the Lord and His Word."

> WHEN I FELT THAT GOD WAS THROUGH WITH ME, YOU SHOWED ME THAT HE STILL LOVES A PRODIGAL SON.

Jeremy's story is representative of thousands of other lives that we have seen the Lord transform. Our God fixes broken things. He fixes broken lives.

Tina Is Healed of Cancerous Tumors

Some time ago, a dear lady in our church ran up to me, shouting, "Pastor Tiz! Let me tell you what the Lord has done for me!" With tears streaming down her face, Tina told me her wonderful testimony. She reminded me that several weeks before, she had come to me for prayer. At that time, she had told me that she was a two-time cancer survivor. Recently, however, she had been in severe pain for a few weeks, and she finally went to the doctor. During the checkup, he took a number of X-rays that revealed several nodules on her lungs. When he told her that it appeared the cancer had returned, fear assaulted her heart and mind. She had lived through this scenario two times before and was terrified to live through it all over again.

Soon, she calmed herself with the promises of God and chose to believe in His healing power over the report of her doctor.

She came to church as quickly as she could and ran to me for prayer. It was apparent that her fear was strong, but her faith and confession were even stronger. We agreed together in prayer for her miracle of healing, for Jesus said, *"If two of you on earth agree about anything you ask for, it will be done for you by my Father in heaven"* (Matthew 18:19 NIV). The Spirit of God swept over Tina, and the pain that had been so severe immediately left her body. I excitedly told her, "Tina, when you go back to the doctor, he's going to tell you it's nothing!"

> EVERY TIME GOD DOES A MIRACLE FOR US, WE BECOME CONTAGIOUS WITH FAITH. THE THINGS THAT WE HAD ONLY HOPED FOR BEFORE, WE THEN BECOME ASSURED OF!

And that's exactly what happened! She went back to her doctor for another evaluation, and when he looked at the new X-ray, he exclaimed, "Tina, there's nothing there! You are completely healthy! Go home!"

Since that time, Tina and I have prayed together with several other women with cancer, and the Lord has healed them, as well! Every time God does a miracle for us, we become contagious with faith. The things that we had only hoped for before, we then become assured of! What the Lord has done for others, He can do for you.

Faith Is a Never-Ending Journey

The journey of faith is never ending; it's never meant to become stagnant or stale. The more we know, the more we realize there is to know! The Lord wants us literally to take Him at His word. He wants us to grow continually in our knowledge of what He has spoken and promised through the Bible. We are to be bold in laying hold of that which He has said He will do, persistently placing faith-demands on the promises of Scripture.

"The prayer of a righteous man [or woman] *is powerful and effective"* (James 5:16 NIV). I am convinced that more miracles are conceived and

birthed through praying men and women than the world will ever know—on this side of eternity, at least! I can only imagine how amazed we will be when we stand before the Lord in heaven and see all the dots of faith that we connected through prayer and confessions during the time we spent on earth. Let's be sure that we never take for granted this incredible privilege that the Lord has entrusted to us!

You can imagine that over the past thirty-plus years of ministry, Larry and I have seen thousands of miracles of every kind. I love to hear the stories of what the Lord is doing for His children, and I love to share those stories with others to encourage their faith. I hope that the testimonies I've shared will inspire you to reach out in faith for your own miracles!

As we get ready to pray the final part of the Lord's Prayer together, let's refresh our minds with a few important points:

- God is a good God—all the time!
- God is not a hard taskmaster—He's a kind, loving Savior!
- God isn't stingy and tightfisted—He is generous and abundant with blessings!
- God isn't pointing a finger of judgment and accusation at us—He's reaching out a hand to help us!
- We can trust Him and know His will for us by His promises that are in His Word.
- An incredible amount of wonderful promises await you on this journey of prayer. These promises tell us what God wants to do in us, for us, and through us!
- To know Him is to trust Him. To trust Him is to see His miracles naturally flow freely! Remember, when you come to the Lord with a need, don't just seek the miracle; seek the Miracle Worker!
- When we pray, a divine exchange is taking place: our lack of abilities and resources for God's limitless supply of abilities and resources!
- We're not begging Him to do things for us. We're acknowledging who He is and what He has already done for us! We're simply entering into His promises!

♦ We can know Him and His nature by His names. God's names express who He is and what He desires to do in our lives.

Let's Pray!

Father, we give You all praise and glory. You are almighty and everlasting, Alpha and Omega, the Beginning and the End. To You be the glory for the wonderful works You have done in our lives and in the world. We stand in the strength, the courage, and the faith of our Savior, Jesus Christ. Father, we release Your dominion and authority in our lives. Every place where we put the soles of our feet, You will give us dominion. Everything we put our hands to, You will cause to prosper. Father, we thank You that every stored-up blessing is being released into our lives, into our minds, and into our families. We claim and release every generational blessing that should have been ours. Everything that has been held back by the enemy, Lord, release it now through the blood of Jesus Christ. Father, we put our feet down and proclaim that Satan will have no dominion over our thoughts, our families, our schools, our neighborhoods, or our countries.

In the name of Jesus Christ, Father, we release Your dominion in our lives and in every corner of the world. Have Your way, Lord. Nothing but the will of God in our homes, our schools, our jobs, our cities, our states, our countries, our governments, and the entire world. Nothing but Your will and Your dominion. Release into our lives everything that's been held back by the enemy, including joy, happiness, peace, divine health, victory, prosperity, favor, grace, dominion, anointing, and equipping.

Father, we ask You to raise us up to be lights to the world. Let us be beacons of hope to this world. Father, use our lives. We put You on the throne of our lives, and we will keep You there every day of our lives. As You bless us greatly, we will be great blessings to this world. Father, Your name shall be exalted in all the land, and every knee shall bow to You. We lift up Your name in dominion and authority; we glorify You, we magnify You, and we give You all the praise. We worship You, Lord. In Jesus' name, amen.

Now, Give Him Some Praise and Seal It!

Now I want you to just praise Him. Seal what He just did in your life. Come on, lift up your hands to Him! Let Him be real to you right now. If you need deliverance, let Him deliver you right now. Let Him set you free. Allow the Holy Spirit to inhabit your soul and your spirit. Come on and surrender to Him right now.

Father, we praise You. We praise You, Lord. We worship You, Lord. We worship You, Father. We give You all the praise and all the glory, Lord, in Jesus' precious name. Nothing but the will of God in my life, in my mind, in my family, and in my home, in Jesus' name. Amen!

Jesus told His disciples to end their prayers by saying, *"Thine is the kingdom, and the power, and the glory, for ever. Amen"* (Matthew 6:13).

That sounds like the basis of a new beginning to me!

PRAYER AND PROMISE PRINCIPLES

- We should always conclude our prayers by acknowledging God's sovereignty, for when we do this, we show that we're trusting Him to hear our prayers and to deal with our affairs according to His wonderful, divine will.

- An incredible amount of wonderful promises await you on this journey of prayer. These promises tell us what God wants to do in us, for us, and through us!

- God is a good God—all the time!

Conclusion

ONE FINAL PRAYER

My final prayer for you is...

- That all of your prayers come true!
- That as you press toward all your miracles, you will draw closer and closer to the Miracle Worker!
- That as you become more and more blessed, you will become more and more of a blessing!
- That all of God's blessings and promises will be released in you, for you, and through you as you continue along this incredible, miraculous, never-ending journey!

As you begin and continue your journey of prayer, let me encourage you to always remember how much the Lord loves you and wants to be involved in your everyday life. Talk to Him from your heart anytime and anywhere. Always keep an attitude of gratitude and thank Him for all of His blessings—past, present, and future. Don't just bring a list of needs to Him; build a relationship with Him! He is your Father, and He desires to spend time with you. What an incredible privilege!

Start where you are and do what you can. If you don't have an hour to pray, then pray for ten or fifteen minutes. If you can't set aside a long period of uninterrupted time, then pray on the road or in the shower. But start with something! I believe that as you begin to see the amazing results, changes, and miracles, you will be motivated to make a bigger commitment and investment in prayer.

Never look at prayer as a task on your to-do list, but rather as a privilege on your get-to-do list! When you face challenges in life, as we all do, resist the urge to dwell on the problems. Choose to dwell on God's promises! Instead of telling God how big your problems are, tell your problems how big your God is! Rather than focusing on and magnifying the negative circumstances in the world, focus on and magnify the positive promises in the Word!

Remember, our God does not show favoritism. We each have equal access to Him and to His promises. Take the limits off of your perspective of God, and take the limits off of yourself! You can do all things through Christ Jesus. There are no limits and no boundaries!

All of God's blessings and promises are for you on your incredible, amazing, miraculous, never-ending journey!

Please be sure to write to me and share with me all the miracles and breakthroughs that the Lord does for you. I would love to hear from you!

Prayer Guide

Through our journey of prayer, we will:

- Discover how incredible and wonderful our God is, as well as how big He wants to be within us, for us, and through us!

- Develop our relationships and increase our intimacy with God, our Father!

- Declare and establish His will, His promises, and His blessings in every area of our lives!

- Determine to take the limits off of ourselves and off of our perception of God!

Our Father which art in heaven, hallowed be thy name. Thy kingdom come. Thy will be done in earth, as it is in heaven. Give us this day our daily bread. And forgive us our debts, as we forgive our debtors. And lead us not into temptation, but deliver us from evil: for thine is the kingdom, and the power, and the glory, for ever. Amen.
(Matthew 6:9–13)

I. *"Our Father, which art in heaven, hallowed be thy name."*

- Our God is a good, loving, kind, caring, and generous Father.

- We enter into His blessings by praising and worshipping Him.

- God's names reveal His nature. They show us who He wants to be within us, for us, and through us. Speak His names out loud and thank Him for who He already is in your life!
  - Jehovah Tsidkenu: The God who is my righteousness.
  - Jehovah M'Kaddesh: The God who sanctifies me.
  - Jehovah Shalom: The God who fills me with His peace.
  - Jehovah Shammah: The God who is there for whatever I need, whenever I need it.

- Jehovah Rophe: The God who heals me.
- Jehovah Nissi: The God who is my victory and protection.
- Jehovah Rohi: The God who is my shepherd and guide.
- Jehovah Jireh: The God who provides for all my needs.

II. *"Thy kingdom come. Thy will be done in earth, as it is in heaven."*

- Declare by the authority in the name and by the blood of Jesus, "Nothing but the good and perfect will of God today." God's will is for us to have righteousness, peace, joy, divine health, and prosperity!
- Claim these things boldly for:
  - Yourself.
  - Your family (your spouse, your children, and your other relatives).
  - Your church (the pastors ,staff, leadership, church family, and new converts).
  - The world (your schools, neighborhood, city, state, nation, and other nations).

III. *"Give us this day our daily bread."*

- Believe and confess that it is God's will to prosper and bless you. He is a good, compassionate, and benevolent Father!
- Be specific!
- Be tenacious! Be bold before the throne of grace!
- Declare God's promises to bless everything you put your hands to and every place you put the soles of your feet.
- Declare God's grace, favor, equipping, help, and anointing over your life!
- Ask Him to add His super to your natural to release supernatural provision.

◆ Ask the Lord to bless you greatly so that you can be a great blessing to others!

IV. *"Forgive us our debts, as we forgive our debtors."*

◆ Ask God to forgive you of you sins.

◆ Choose to forgive others and release them to God.

◆ Choose to let go of anger and resentment. Ask the Lord to help you.

◆ Choose to walk in love, compassion, and forgiveness.

◆ Put on joy, peace, love, kindness, and faith.

V. *"Lead us not into temptation, but deliver us from evil."*

◆ Be a mighty warrior dressed for battle.

◆ *"Loins girt about with truth"* (Ephesians 6:14).

  • I declare that the Word of God is true and that all God has promised will be reproduced in my life through Jesus Christ.

◆ *"The breastplate of righteousness"* (Ephesians 6:14).

  • I am the righteous through the blood of Jesus.

  • I will continue to walk in righteousness to protect my heart from the enemy.

◆ *"Feet shod with the preparation of the gospel of peace"* (Ephesians 6:15).

  • I will stand, act, talk, and look like a victorious Christian.

  • I will be ready and proud to tell all who will hear that Jesus is the reason for my joy and victory.

◆ *"Above all, taking the shield of faith"* (Ephesians 6:16).

  • Over all my life, I have faith that Jesus will cause me to be victorious.

  • All things work together for good! (See Romans 8:28.)

  • Every fiery dart will be put out in Jesus' name.

- ◆ *"The helmet of salvation"* (Ephesians 6:17).
  - I plead the blood of Jesus over my mind.
  - No negative, doubting, or impure thoughts will enter my mind.
- ◆ *"The sword of the Spirit, which is the word of God"* (Ephesians 6:17).
  - I will put a guard on my mouth today.
  - I will pray it before I say it, for my words are spirit and therefore have creative powers.
  - I will let nothing but the Word of God come from my mouth today.
- ◆ Pray a hedge of spiritual protection...
  - Around you, your family, your church, and your pastors.
  - You are the church of Jesus Christ, and the gates of hell cannot prevail against you.

VI. *"For thine is the kingdom, and the power, and the glory, for ever. Amen."*

- ◆ Praise the Lord and tell Him that you love Him!
- ◆ Thank Him for His grace, favor, and help!
- ◆ Seal your prayers with worship, praise, and thanksgiving!

About the Author

Tiz Huch

Tiz Huch copastors DFW New Beginnings in Irving, Texas, with her husband, Pastor Larry Huch. Founded in November 2004, this non-denominational church has quickly developed into a diverse, multiethnic congregation of several thousand people. Pastors Larry and Tiz are driven by a passionate commitment to see people succeed in every area of life. That passion, along with their enthusiasm, genuine love for people, and effective teaching, has fueled a ministry that spans more than thirty years and two continents.

That same energy and commitment to sharing a positive, life-changing, and biblically based message with the world is the hallmark of Pastors Larry and Tiz's international television program, *New Beginnings*. This program is broadcast weekly to millions of homes around the globe and has served to touch and change the lives of countless people worldwide.

As the successful author of several books and teaching series, Tiz is a frequent speaker at seminars and conferences throughout the world. Her teachings on prayer, in particular, have changed the lives of countless people. She is an inspiring and insightful communicator with vast experience and passion in the areas of ministry and business. She has a unique anointing to communicate in a way that is both personal and practical, and her teaching focuses on living the abundant life in marriage, family, personal relationships, business, and finances.

With a passion to inspire women to be all that God has created them to be, Tiz created the Women's Business Network to promote the entrepreneurial pursuits of Christian women. Tiz is also a recognized and accomplished artist whose faith-based artwork is featured in many galleries and retail venues.

Pastors Larry and Tiz are both wholeheartedly committed to bridging the gap between Christians and Jews and restoring the church to its Judeo-Christian roots. Pastor Larry had the honor of speaking at the Israeli Knesset, and the two have received awards from the Knesset Social Welfare Lobby for their generosity toward the needs of the Jewish people in Israel.

Pastors Larry and Tiz are the proud parents of three wonderful children (and a terrific son-in-law and daughter-in-law), all of whom are active in ministry. Their three grandchildren, the "Sugars," are the loves of their lives!